TEACHERS' RESOURCES

Practical Tips for New
TEACHERS

WATERBIRD BOOKS
Columbus, Ohio

President: Vincent F. Douglas
Publisher: Tracey E. Dils
Contributor: Sue O'Connell
Project Editors: Joanna Callihan, Teresa Domnauer
Interior Design and Production: Lithokraft

 **Children's Publishing**

This edition published in the United States in 2003 by Waterbird Books,
an imprint of McGraw-Hill Children's Publishing,
A Division of The McGraw-Hill Companies
8787 Orion Place
Columbus, Ohio 43240-4027

www.MHkids.com

Library of Congress Cataloging-in-Publication Data is on file with the publisher.

Printed in the United States of America.

1-57768-538-5

1 2 3 4 5 6 7 8 9 10 PHXBK 09 08 07 06 05 04 03

The McGraw-Hill Companies

Table of Contents

Chapter 1: Designing Your Classroom 5

Chapter 2: Starting Off on the Right Foot 11

Chapter 3: Organizing Your Classroom with Clear Rules and Procedures 21

Chapter 4: Managing Student Behavior 32

Chapter 5: Developing Relations with Students, Staff, and Parents 39

Chapter 6: Planning, Delivering, and Assessing Instruction 44

Chapter 7: Special and Unexpected Events 54

Chapter 8: Reflecting on the Joys and Challenges of Teaching 62

Chapter 9: Activity Ideas to Get You Started 67

Index 94

A Note to New Teachers

You have chosen a career with endless joys and daily challenges. Your first year will be busy and filled with many new experiences. This book is designed to help you through that first year. From decorating your classroom, to planning lessons, to establishing classroom rules, to getting ready for that first day, you will find a myriad of tips, strategies, and practical ideas that will help you through your first year and for many years to come.

While this book will help you get organized and ready to start the year, it will also be an ongoing resource for you. Keep this book close at hand and refer to it as you need assistance. You will find reproducibles to make your job a little easier, checklists to remind you of important tasks, and many practical tips from master teachers who share their knowledge and experience with you.

Hopefully, this book will provide you with the support you need for a successful first year. By guiding you through the many daily responsibilities of a classroom teacher, it will free you to focus on your students and their learning.

Enjoy your new career!

Sincerely,
Waterbird Books

Chapter 1
Designing Your Classroom

Make Learning the Central Focus of Your Classroom

You will be taking an empty room and transforming it into a classroom environment that is welcoming and attractive. Your room should be inviting to students, making them feel safe and welcome. And most importantly, your room should be designed to promote learning for all of your students. The decisions you make about where to place furniture, how to decorate the walls and bulletin boards, where to situate key instructional areas, and where to store important instructional materials will guide you in transforming your empty room into an exciting learning environment.

1 Make Your Classroom Attractive and Motivating

Bring color and fun into your classroom by decorating walls and bulletin boards in bright, colorful, and age-appropriate ways. But be careful not to overdecorate! Wall space completely filled with posters, pictures, and schoolwork can be overwhelming and over-stimulating for some students.

If you have a shortage of wall space on which to hang posters or student work, consider the following options: use paper clips to attach papers to blinds, use yarn or string to create a clothesline and attach student work with clothespins, or hang pictures or student art from the ceiling with string or yarn.

Instill the love of reading in your students by creating an attractive library area in your classroom. Gather books from family and friends, ask for donations of used books from parents, buy books at yard sales, or join classroom book clubs to earn free books. Be sure to display books to entice your students to read.

2 Create Bulletin Boards That Motivate and Teach

Bulletin boards play an important role in your classroom décor, but it is important for bulletin boards to be more than just decorations. Bulletin boards serve two purposes: to make your room more attractive and to support classroom activities. You may decide to have a Student of the Week board to build self-esteem or a Math Word Wall to reinforce important math vocabulary. Bulletin boards may reinforce recent lessons or remind students of essential basic skills.

Displaying student work personalizes your classroom. It helps your students see pieces of themselves as they look around your room. You may choose to display weekly spelling papers or to create a bulletin board that allows students to choose and display pieces of work of which they are proud.

Making bulletin boards can be a chore or a delight! Learn the shortcuts to make the task easier. Talk to or observe experienced teachers to see their ideas for lessening the "chore" of bulletin boards. For example:

• Project a graphic on the wall with an overhead projector and then trace the outline of the object on a large piece of paper taped to the wall. Color and cut out the object for a bulletin-board-sized graphic.

- Some schools have machines that punch out letters and numbers; sets can also be purchased at local teacher stores. Gradually collect and keep several sets of each letter (upper- and lowercase) of the alphabet for spelling out bulletin board titles. Laminate the letters for durability.

- When creating your own set of letters, laminate the paper prior to cutting. This will allow you to reuse the letters throughout the year for a variety of bulletin board titles. Cut out about five of each letter.

- Use thumb tacks to hold the backing paper in place while you straighten or smooth it out; then staple it when you are satisfied with how it looks. Temporarily thumbtacking letters or graphics on the board will allow you to move and experiment with the arrangement before stapling it.

Don't try to do everything yourself! Go to teacher stores for ready-made materials with which to decorate your classroom. Your colleagues have had years to collect and create the many decorations around their rooms. Little by little you can create original items for your room, but don't try to do it all at once.

3 Anticipate Problems and Arrange Your Room to Minimize Them

When students are in your room, your goal is to have them focus on your instruction. Limit distractions to allow students to concentrate on the task of learning.

Avoid traffic jams in your classroom! Identify a traffic pattern that allows students to move throughout the room without congestion occurring. If students' desks are somewhat close together, you could have them walk around the outer area of the classroom or down designated aisles when entering or leaving the room.

Designating a traffic pattern will prevent students from moving through the room in random directions and will also prevent student traffic jams that may inevitably result in behavior problems.

As students need to move throughout the room, be sure that there is ample room for them to get past furniture and other students. Set up supplies and student work areas (centers, computers, library area, textbook shelves) where students can easily get to them.

Carefully consider the placement of trash cans, pencil sharpeners, pets, or other distractions. And don't forget that students often distract each other. If students are seated in teams/groups, try to limit teams to five or fewer students. Consider whether you have placed students' desks too close to areas where other students may be working (a reading group area, computer workstation, or learning center). Be sure that students know your expectations and the consequences for talking to or playing with other team members.

4 Be Sure That Each Student Has Personal Space

Allowing each student some personal space will eliminate many potential problems. Be sure that each child has a place to store supplies, hang a coat, and keep his or her lunch. If space is limited, set up a system for storing items, possibly labeling each coat hook with a child's name. Seat students so that they have some personal space and are not too close to each other.

Will all of your students' supplies fit into their desks? If not, they will need a space for some personal belongings. If cubicles are not available, each child can bring a shoebox or plastic tote from home. You may also search the local dollar stores to find inexpensive containers for each student. Label each student's bin with his or her name.

5 Choose a Seating Arrangement That Makes the Best Use of Available Space

Choosing an appropriate seating arrangement is an important classroom decision. Will your students be doing a lot of group work? Will they frequently be asked to share with a partner? Early in the year, you may want to begin with a more traditional seating arrangement that keeps students' eyes on you. Later, after the rules and procedures are understood, you may want to move students' desks into groups, forming "tables," to allow for partner and group activities without moving furniture.

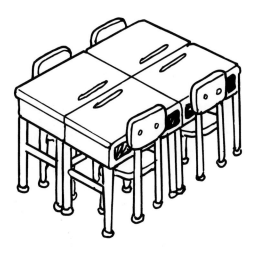

When seating students in groups, put each student's name on a small index card. Use the index cards to model seating arrangements. Change card positions until you are satisfied with a seating arrangement. Be sure to consider behavior concerns and students' academic abilities when arranging your groups.

Change student seating periodically. Keep students motivated and on task by providing them with new environments throughout the year. Sitting in a different part of the room, with a different group of students, will keep them on their toes!

Will you be doing any small group instruction? If so, plan where you might locate the small group. Will you place a table and chairs at the back of the room? Will you ask students to bring their chairs to an open area in the classroom? Will you rearrange seating throughout the day, so that students who are in your group will be seated together? Do you need a rug and open floor space for students to sit on? Does your small group area have a bulletin board, overhead projector, or chart paper to allow for visual lessons?

Finally, where will your desk be located? Keep it away from high student traffic areas. Be careful not to place student materials or supplies behind or next to your desk. Your desk does not need to be in front of the room—remember, it is your workspace, not a place from which to deliver instruction!

6 Have a Plan for Keeping Your Room Clean and Interesting

Design your bulletin boards to be easily changed. For example, you may change posted work or have a science bulletin board on which the topics are changed as new units are introduced. Backing your boards with fabric or nonfading bulletin board paper will allow you to change the items on the board without redoing the backing.

Start clean and keep it clean. Have students help you with room cleanup. There are many jobs that they can do to help keep your room clean and uncluttered, including dusting shelves or computers, picking up trash, cleaning blackboards, and straightening desks.

Keep your desk clean and organized. You are modeling good habits for your students. Provide incentives for students to keep their own desks clean. You may want to leave notes on clean desks or periodically leave small treats in clean desks. It's best to do this unannounced, so that students never know when you might check their desks.

DESIGNING YOUR CLASSROOM

Occasionally, whole class cleanups may be needed. Establish a system for this, or the process can be chaotic, with students dumping desk contents onto the floor or moving all around the room to throw away trash! First, ask students to stack their books on their desk tops and then to pull out any trash. Finally, have a student or two travel systematically around the room with a trash can. Explaining the procedures before you begin will keep the room calm during the cleanup.

7 Design a Classroom That Makes Your Students Feel like Part of the Class

Your students need to see your classroom as "home" for the next year—a place where they belong. Help them see themselves in your classroom. Be sure that the decorations you choose are age and grade level appropriate and reflect the diversity of students in your room. Put name tags on students' desks and include students' names on bulletin boards and helper charts.

Post student work throughout the classroom. Allow students to choose a "best work" paper to display. Create a *We're Proud of Our Work* bulletin board with space for each student to display a work sample of which he or she is particularly proud. After covering your bulletin board with backing paper, use yarn to create a rectangle for each student in the class. Then label each rectangle with a student's name. Add a border to the bulletin board and the heading *We're Proud of Our Work*. Every few weeks, encourage students to change their work samples on display.

We're Proud of Our Work

Joe · Rita · Jamel · Erica · Steven · Michael
Maria · Brendan · Colleen · James · Kevin · Li
Grace · Katie · Andrew · Melissa · Megan · Ryan
Miguel · LaShawn · Kathy · Antonio · Lisa · Dan

Tips from Teachers. . .

"At the beginning of the year, I face students toward me so all of their eyes are on me. Then, once they know the rules and procedures in my class, I put them into groups."

"I put tape on the floor to show my primary students where to sit during story time."

"Before the students arrive, I sit in different spots in my room and read the posters and charts to be sure the printing is large enough for students to see."

"I put an extra desk in my class, so that if a new student joins us he or she can be seated immediately and feel more a part of the class."

"Decorate a bulletin board in your classroom with the word *SUPPLIES*. Then, actually hang up the supplies: backpack, pencils, composition book, crayons, etc. This is good for your visual learners and your parent visitors, too. At the end of September, take it down, put the supplies in the backpack, zip it up, and store it in your closet until next September—EASY!"

"I decorate some of my bulletin boards before the students arrive, but I always leave one or two for displaying first-day activities. I put the backing paper, border, and heading on the board before they arrive, and then complete it with their first day art work or writing."

"I create an *I Can* bulletin board. I have each student write or illustrate something he or she can do."

"I create a large sample of a proper paper heading (name, date, subject) and display it where all students can see it; that way they all know what I expect."

KEYS TO
Designing Your Classroom

Use the checklist below to see if your classroom passes the "Ready to Start the Year" test.

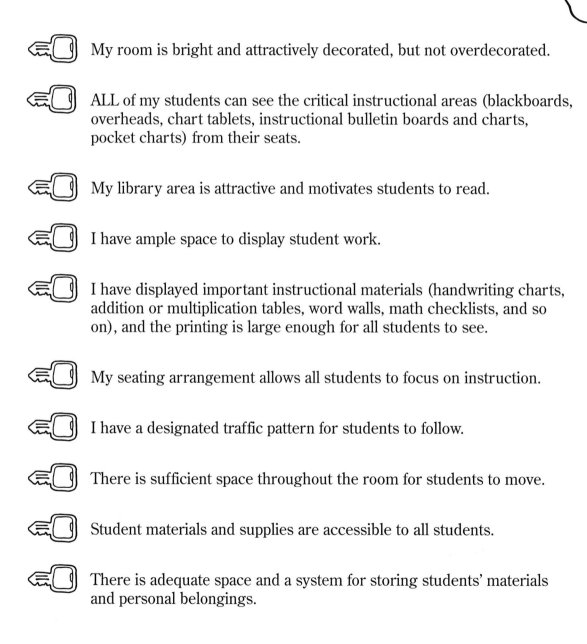

My room is bright and attractively decorated, but not overdecorated.

ALL of my students can see the critical instructional areas (blackboards, overheads, chart tablets, instructional bulletin boards and charts, pocket charts) from their seats.

My library area is attractive and motivates students to read.

I have ample space to display student work.

I have displayed important instructional materials (handwriting charts, addition or multiplication tables, word walls, math checklists, and so on), and the printing is large enough for all students to see.

My seating arrangement allows all students to focus on instruction.

I have a designated traffic pattern for students to follow.

There is sufficient space throughout the room for students to move.

Student materials and supplies are accessible to all students.

There is adequate space and a system for storing students' materials and personal belongings.

Chapter 2
Starting Off on the Right Foot

Plan Thoroughly for the First Days

The first days of school are filled with new and exciting activities. Be sure to plan carefully for the first few days, keeping in mind that unexpected events (a new student assigned to your class, a crying child, a missed bus, or forgotten lunches) are sure to happen. Be prepared in every way possible and then with flexibility and humor do your best to deal with whatever the first days bring. Keep in mind that your enthusiasm and calmness will rub off on the students who enter your classroom. Above all else, provide your students with a positive start to the school year!

1 Am I in the Right Class?

Eliminate students' fears of being in the wrong room by posting a class list outside your classroom. Put name tags on the students' desks. Students might be asked to color their name tags as a warm-up on the first day. Laminating name tags before taping them to the desks will help them last longer. The name tags will help you quickly learn students' names and will be a great help to other staff who enter the room to work with your students.

Have an extra desk in your room and extra copies of any handouts. You never know when an additional student might be added to your class!

Plan a warm-up activity for students to do independently each morning of the first week. Post the activity on the blackboard or place a worksheet on each student's desk. Consider the morning tasks that you will be doing for the first few days of school and select a warm-up activity that will engage the students long enough for you to complete your tasks.

2 Have a Supply List Ready for Students

Some schools have supply lists that are agreed upon by grade level teams; in other schools, supplies are different for each class. Check with your principal to see if an existing list is available. If you have to generate your own supply list, check with a colleague at the same grade level to see which supplies he/she requests from parents. Prepare a supply list to send home on the first day of school. Be as specific as possible (What kind of paper? How many crayons? What type of glue, liquid or stick?). Decide where you will place the supplies when they are brought to school. You may want to collect some items and store them in a central place, as they may not fit in your students' desks or may distract students.

Keep in mind that it may take a few days (or longer) for students to bring in their supplies, so design first week activities that can be done with few supplies or with supplies that you can provide.

3 Get Ready for the Paperwork!

Lots of papers go back and forth between class and home during the first few days! Check with the office to be sure that you are aware of all necessary paperwork.

Your school will have a procedure for getting emergency phone numbers. Once students return these forms to you, send copies to the office and keep copies for yourself. It's always a good idea to leave copies of student phone numbers at home and at school. That way, you will always have them when you need them!

Make multiple copies of your class list (see *Class List* on page 20) so that you can grab a copy when needed; for example, to note which students returned papers, brought in supplies, completed homework, or brought field trip money. Having several copies of the class list will be especially important during the first week, when you need to monitor which students have returned the necessary papers from home.

4 Getting Students Home on the First Day

Start preparing your class for dismissal early! Leave yourself plenty of time to get students ready to go home. They may need to pack up backpacks, locate paperwork to bring home, or maybe even copy down homework. Allow extra time to prepare for dismissal; then have a story ready to read to the class if you finish early.

Be sure that you know how each student gets to and from school. You will want to get this information early in the day so that you can check with the office if dismissal plans are unclear for any child in your room. Have a class list with transportation instructions for each student on it with you during the first day's dismissal, so that you can be sure that all students get on the right buses or get dismissed with the correct group. After school, post the names of walkers, bus riders, and car riders on your classroom door or bulletin board where you can easily see them at daily dismissal.

5 Establish Your Classroom Rules and Procedures

Right from the very first day, your students need to know what you expect of them. Talk about the behaviors that are appropriate in your classroom. Repeat yourself frequently. Allow time to discuss the classroom rules with your students; be sure that they understand the meaning of each rule. You may want to roleplay or just talk about what each rule means and how you will know when students are following the rules. A detailed discussion for establishing classroom rules and procedures takes place in Chapter 3.

6 Get to Know Your Students

Be warm and welcoming as your students enter your classroom. First impressions are strong and enduring. Learn each student's name as quickly as possible. Calling students by their names will help make them feel welcome. Share something about yourself and plan some get-to-know-you activities to help your students learn about each other. You might ask students to write poems about themselves (see the *Poetry Fun* activities on page 19, or have them interview each other about their favorite things). Create some class graphs about topics such as students' favorite snack foods, number of people in their families, ways they get to school, favorite summer fruits, favorite summer activities, favorite subjects in school, or favorite breakfasts. Give students time to share the information they discovered with the class; then display their creations in the room.

7 Assess Your Students' Abilities

During the first weeks, plan activities that will allow you to assess your students' strengths and weaknesses. Short mixed math reviews of skills taken from the previous year's textbook will tell you what your students remember and what they may have forgotten. Observing your students read or reviewing their writing skills will provide you with valuable information with which to start the year. Most students will benefit greatly from reviewing basic skills such as math facts, problem solving strategies, letter writing techniques, and map reading, etc. The first few weeks are a time to observe your students, assess their skills, provide the necessary review lessons to "remind" them of any forgotten skills, and build a strong foundation for the many new skills to be learned in the year ahead.

8 Select a Story to Read to the Class

Develop a love of reading in your students! Read aloud to students often. This will excite them about reading and show your love for reading. Younger students love to look through the pictures in a book or reread the stories you have read to them. With older students, you might begin reading the first few chapters of a book and then place it in your library area so that students may finish on their own. Read the first book in a series and then tell students about the others. Read-alouds are a great way to develop students' background knowledge before beginning a science or social studies unit and are a great way to begin class discussion about a variety of topics. Read-alouds also provide you with opportunities for first-week activities. Students can be asked to illustrate scenes from the story, describe the setting or characters, predict coming events, or write their own endings to the story. See the list of *Books to Read Aloud* on page 18 for good books with a Back-to-School theme.

Tips from Teachers. . .

On Getting to Know Each Other

"I stand at the door and greet my students as they enter each morning. As I know more about them I try to make a personal comment like "Did you have soccer practice yesterday?" or "How does your little brother like kindergarten?""

"On the first day, I send a welcome letter home to parents, telling them how happy I am to have their children in my class for the year and how much I am looking forward to the year."

"I prepare a presentation about myself. I supplement it with pictures, objects, maps, etc. I have them prepare a presentation about themselves. I let them select the type of presentation—it does not have to be an oral presentation."

"We sit in a big circle and roll a ball around, and whoever has the ball gets to tell the class his or her name, favorite food, and favorite thing he or she did at school that day."

"I learn names immediately and try to call students by their names at all times."

"I assign student helpers from the first day. I explain each job and rotate the jobs each day, so that by the end of the first week everyone has had a job and feels like part of the class."

"I take pictures of my students and hang them on the walls of the room."

"I ask each student to say his or her name and something that he or she does well (a strength), so that from the first day, everyone knows something positive about each person in the class."

On the First Week's Activities

"I keep a "first week folder" with all of my ideas for week number one."

"Lots of papers go home with students on the first few days of school. I lay them all out so that I don't forget any and make myself a checklist of which are being sent home when."

"I always have an extra activity available that students can do independently, just in case I have to deal with an unexpected situation."

Tips from Teachers. . .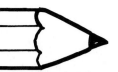

On the First Week's Activities (continued)

"Always give work that you are sure everyone can do on the first day."

"I do some quick end-of-year checks from the previous grade to see where my students are academically. This helps me get an idea of how well they mastered last year's material, and how quickly I can move through new material."

On Managing Supplies

"I collect some supplies, like glue or scissors. That way, students don't have them in their desks to play with during class. When we are using glue, I take out my basket of glue and distribute it to the students."

"I have a supply form to send home to parents when students do not have what they need. It is a list of supplies, and I have students circle their missing items. This is sent home to alert parents to what they need to send to school."

"I number textbooks and record the number given to each student. The student is responsible for that book throughout the year."

"I introduce new textbooks with a Textbook Treasure Hunt. I give students some items to find in their textbooks, and we review the parts of a book (glossary, index, table of contents) that might help them locate the items. Some sample questions for a math textbook might include

• What is a polygon?
• In which chapter will we learn about fractions?
• On which pages will we read about right angles?

With the Textbook Treasure Hunt, students get an introduction to what they will be learning throughout the year, and we get a chance to review some important reading skills."

"I always have some extras of important supplies. I have extra pencils that students can sign out from me to borrow for the day. I always keep a basket of crayons; some are broken or old ones, but they work when a child doesn't have any!"

"I always specify the size/quantity for supplies (for example, pack of eight crayons). This is helpful so that students don't bring in the 64 pack, which often doesn't fit in their desks!"

"I cover my softcover books with clear contact paper so they last longer. This is especially helpful for books that are in students' hands a lot."

KEYS TO
A Successful Start

Use the checklist below to see if you are ready to welcome your students on that first day.

- I have multiple copies of my most current class list.

- I have the day's schedule on the board.

- My first day warmup can be done independently, is interesting, and will take some time to complete.

- I have a plan for taking attendance and lunch count.

- I know which students are bus riders, car riders, or walkers, and I have a plan to record that information early in the day so that I am ready for dismissal.

- I have supplies for students to use for the first few days until they bring their own.

- I have thought about important procedures and am ready to share them with my students.

- I have a get-to-know-you activity planned so that I can begin to learn about my students and they can begin to learn about each other.

- I have all paperwork that must be sent home (supply lists, welcome letter, emergency information cards, and so on) sorted and ready to distribute.

- I have all books stacked and ready to distribute, and all papers copied and ready to distribute.

- I have a captivating story to read to the class.

- I have books available for students to read.

Handy Sponge Activities to Soak Up Those Extra Minutes

Need a quick activity? Maybe you have five or ten minutes before your class has to line up for lunch, or maybe you need a few minutes to get a new student settled into your classroom. Have your students try one of the following activities. Choose the prompt that fits your students' ages and abilities.

Draw a picture of a pet you would like to have.

Draw a picture of your family.

Draw a picture to show 4 + 2 = 6 (or any appropriate number sentence).

List words that begin with the letters in your first name.

List words that begin with *st* (or any beginning sound).

List tame animals and wild animals.

Make a list of fruits and vegetables.

List workers in the city and workers in the country.

List people who work during the day and people who work at night.

Make a list of opposites.

List words with double consonants in them (for example, *ladder, kettle, better*).

List creatures that live in a forest habitat.

List cities in your state.

List number sentences that equal 16 (for example, 10 + 6 = 16 or 20 − 4 = 16).

List items found on a map.

Make a list of things that will help you stay healthy.

List things that a teacher does.

List times when knowing fractions is helpful.

List times when you need to measure.

Name the states in the United States.

Name famous inventors.

List people who lived in Revolutionary times.

Name the presidents of the United States.

List things you might see in a desert.

List words relating to the weather.

Name rivers in the United States.

List things that harm the environment.

List probability words.

Name countries in Europe.

Books to Read Aloud

Books for Younger Students

Annabelle Swift, Kindergartner by Amy Schwartz (Orchard Books, 1991)

Are There Any Questions? by Denys Cazet (Orchard Books, 1998)

Cleversticks. by Bernard Ashley (Crown Books for Young Readers, 1995)

Double Trouble in Walla Walla by Andrew Clements (Millbrook Press, 1997)

Emily's First 100 Days of School by Rosemary Wells (Hyperion, 2000)

Froggy Goes to School by Jonathan London (Penguin Putnam, 1996)

How The Second Grade Got $8,205.50 to Visit the Statue of Liberty by Nathan Zimelman
  (Albert Whitman & Co., 1992)

Lilly's Purple Plastic Purse by Kevin Henkes (William Morrow & Co., 1996)

The Lunch Line by Karen Berman Nagel (Scholastic, 1996)

Miss Nelson is Back by Harry Allard and James Marshall (Houghton Mifflin, 1982)

Miss Nelson is Missing! by Harry Allard and James Marshall (Houghton Mifflin, 1977)

The Night Before Kindergarten by Natasha Wing (Grosset & Dunlap, 2001)

Officer Buckle and Gloria by Peggy Rathmann (G.P. Putnam & Sons, 1995)

Rachel Parker, Kindergarten Show-Off by Ann M. Martin (Holiday House, 1993)

School Days by B.G. Hennessy (Penguin USA, 1992)

Sheila Rae, the Brave by Kevin Henkes (William Morrow & Co., 1996)

Today Was a Terrible Day by Patricia Reilly Giff (Viking Children's Books, 1980)

Wemberly Worried by Kevin Henkes (Greenwillow Books, 2000)

Books for Older Students

Aldo Applesauce by Johanna Hurwitz (Penguin Putnam, 1991)

First Day Jitters by Julie Danneberg (Charlesbridge, 2000)

Fourth Grade Rats by Jerry Spinelli (Scholastic, 1993)

Horrible Harry in Room 2B by Suzy Kline (Penguin Putnam, 1997)

Judy Moody by Megan McDonald (Candlewick, 2000)

Junie B. Jones and the Stupid Smelly Bus by Barbara Park (Random House, 1992)

Marvin Redpost: Alone in His Teacher's House by Louis Sachar (Random House, 1992)

Math Curse by Jon Scieszka and Lane Smith (Viking, 1995)

Muggie Maggie by Beverly Cleary (William Morrow & Co., 1991)

Oliver Pig at School by Jean Van Leeuwan (Penguin Putnam Books, 1994)

Ramona Quimby, Age 8 by Beverly Cleary (William Morrow & Co., 1992)

Sideways Stories from Wayside School by Louis Sachar (William Morrow & Co., 1985)

Sixth Grade Can Really Kill You by Barthe DeClements (Penguin Putnam Books for Young Readers, 1994)

Tales of a Fourth Grade Nothing by Judy Blume (Bantam Doubleday Dell, 1976)

Teach Us, Amelia Bedelia by Peggy Parish (Scholastic, 1995)

There's a Boy in the Girls' Bathroom by Louis Sachar (Random House, 1997)

Poetry Fun Activity

Have students share something about themselves through poetry. Try one of these fun activities. Parents will love to read students' poems on Back-to-School Night!

Couplets

See if students can tell about themselves in two lines that rhyme.

Erica likes to play in the pool.
She always listens to her teacher in school.

Triplets

Have students add a third line and make all three lines rhyme.

Megan kicks a soccer ball.
She plays soccer in the fall.
Her sister is little, and her father is tall.

Cinquain

Students can describe themselves in a cinquain, following these guidelines:

1 noun
2 adjectives
3 verbs
4 word phrase
1 noun

Joe
Athletic, smart
Passing, dribbling, scoring
Loves to play basketball
Friend

For older students, challenge them to create cinquains based on syllables, rather than just the number of words in each line. Lines should have the following:

2 syllables (noun)
4 syllables (adjectives)
6 syllables (verbs)
8 syllables (descriptive phrase)
2 syllables (noun)

Acrostic Poems

Acrostic poems express ideas in words or phrases that begin with the letters in students' names.

***S**ports enthusiast*
***A**ctive*
***M**ischievous at times*

***S**its in the front of the class*
***M**ath is his favorite*
***I**s funny*
***T**alks a lot at recess*
***H**as one brother*

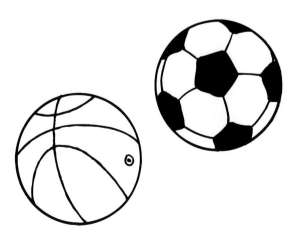

Class List

Class List										

Chapter 3
Organizing Your Classroom with Clear Rules and Procedures

Create Classroom Rules That Your Students Understand

Students will be more likely to remember and follow your rules if they are involved in making them. Instead of starting the year with rules already posted on your wall, involve your students in a discussion of the rules that would be necessary for your classroom to run smoothly throughout the year. Do students need to treat each other nicely? Do students need to respect each other's property? Do students need to follow the teacher's directions?

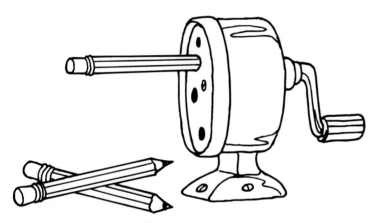

When posting your rules, use language that your students understand. While fifth graders may understand "Treat others with respect," first graders may simply say "Treat others nicely" or "Treat others like you want them to treat you." Some schools have schoolwide rules that are posted throughout the building. If this is the case in your school, go over the language with your students and be sure that they understand what each rule means. Even very young students can talk about how they like to be treated. Acting out scenarios relating to the rules and discussing how students should behave in each scenario will help students better understand the rules. Asking students to describe what "respect" or "following directions" looks like or sounds like will allow students to see the rules in concrete ways.

1 **Tips for Establishing Class Rules**
- Have just a few rules (four or five is plenty).
- Involve students in making the rules.
- Use language that your students understand.
- Share your rules with parents.

2 **Decide on Procedures for All of the Daily Tasks That Students Will Be Asked to Do**
In just one school day, students are involved in countless tasks that can be done either in an organized way or in a way that creates confusion and chaos within your classroom. Even for the simplest tasks, such as sharpening pencils and passing in papers, students need to know what you expect of them. Consider some of the following questions:

- When students want to answer a question, should they call out, or raise their hand?
- If students need to ask you a question, should they walk up to your desk?
- What if students need to use the restroom? Do they need your permission? Do they need a pass?
- Should students get a drink of water during class?
- If a student's pencil breaks during the math lesson, should he or she get up and sharpen it?
- How will students line up to leave your classroom?
- Do they need to be silent when walking through the hallways?
- What if a student is absent—does he or she need to complete the work that was missed?

Do you have an answer for each of these questions? Your classroom will run more smoothly if you, and your students, know the answers.

3 Establish Procedures That Work for You

There is more than one way to manage a classroom. Decide on the procedures that will work for your classroom. Make sure that your students know these procedures. Some teachers use bathroom passes, others have a signout sheet, and others require students to get permission directly from them. If the procedure is consistently enforced, the behavior becomes automatic.

In deciding on your procedures, think of a task, such as sharpening pencils. Now, consider the problems that could result if you had no procedures in place. Keeping potential problems that might arise in mind, decide on procedures for sharpening pencils. Consider the following examples:

Problem	Procedure
Too many students in line	No more than three students in line at a time
One student sharpening 20 pencils	Sharpen two or fewer pencils
Students grinding pencils at the sharpener during a lesson	Pencil sharpener is open only from 8 to 8:20 a.m.
Students opening the sharpener and attempting to dump the shavings	Assign a helper who dumps shavings

Now you have determined a procedure that may prevent problems from occurring! Follow the same process to determine a procedure for each issue in your classroom.

4 Teach Your Procedures and Then Consistently Reinforce Them

Procedures must be taught and consistently reinforced. Explain your procedures and post them whenever possible. A note such as the following by the pencil sharpener might remind students of your procedure.

Pencil Sharpener Hours
8:00–8:20 a.m.
You may sharpen up to two pencils today!
Remember only three students in line at a time!

If the shavings are full, notify our helper.

For some procedures, students may need to practice several times before mastering what you expect of them. Walking down the halls, for example may take much longer at the beginning of the year, as you move slowly, stop frequently, and remind students of what you expect.

Be sure that you have a consequence in mind when students forget to follow a procedure. Consequences should be logical and remind everyone that you are serious about this procedure. If there are four people in line at the pencil sharpener, ask the last one to sit back down. If a student takes five pencils to the pencil sharpener, ask him or her to go back to his seat and put the extra three pencils in his or her desk. If a student gets up to sharpen a pencil, remind him or her that the pencil sharpener is closed and allow him or her to borrow a pencil from you. Consistently enforcing your procedures will remind students of what you expect. Soon, procedures will become automatic for your students, and you will have an organized classroom and more time to spend on teaching!

Periodically throughout the year, ask yourself this question:

- Do I consistently enforce procedures?

- When my line is noisy in the hallways, do I remind students what I expect?

- When a student calls out without raising his hand, do I answer him?

- When a student races to beat another student to the line, do I react?

- When a student gets out of his or her seat to ask me a question, do I answer it?

5 Essentials for Teaching Procedures

- Tell students what you expect. Give them all of the details!

- Show them what you expect. Practice the task with them until they've got it!

- Remind them what you expect. Stay alert! Consistently reinforce the procedure.

6 Organize the Start of the Day and Begin Each Day Calmly

Have a daily schedule and follow it. Students respond to structure. Put your schedule on the blackboard or laminate a daily schedule poster and write the specifics of each day with erasable washable marker. Read the schedule to your students each morning to prepare them for the events of the day.

Have an activity waiting for students as they enter each morning. Select an activity that reviews a previously taught skill or sets the stage for an activity that students will be involved in during the day. After students have completed the morning activity, correct it with them. Many teachers move around the room during the review to monitor whether all students complete the task. Others collect the already corrected work to be sure that each student has completed it.

7 Organize the End of Your Day

End each day calmly. Consider the tasks that your students will need to do at this time. Will they be getting coats and packing backpacks? Will they need to copy homework, wash blackboards, or straighten desks? Will they need to return any books or supplies to storage areas? Will they need to have these tasks completed before afternoon announcements? Be sure that students know the procedures. Allow enough time to end the day calmly, with a summary of the day's activities and a look ahead to tomorrow's activities.

8 Be Aware of Students during Transitions

Many behavior problems begin when students are uninvolved in lessons. Give specific directions for transition times. After completing the reading lesson, you might ask students to (1) put away their reading books, (2) take out their math books, a sheet of paper, and pencils, (3) put headings on the paper, and (4) put their pencils down and look at you to show that they are done. By giving specific directions and then monitoring students during transitions, you will eliminate talking and playing among students. Being able to monitor student transitions is only possible, however, if you are completely prepared to move to the next subject. If your materials are ready, you can keep your eyes and ears focused on your students.

9 Be Prepared!

Have your schedule posted before you go home each day; leave your plan book on your desk. Stack the materials you will need (teacher's guides, worksheets, overhead transparencies, and so on) in one spot, near your instructional area. If your day ever starts with an unexpected meeting or an unexpected parent phone call, preparation in advance will allow you to step right into your classroom and begin the day without a problem.

Always have extra supplies (such as pencils, scissors, crayons, glue, paper) on hand. Be sure that students have no excuse for not completing their assignments.

Have a procedure for passing out and collecting work.

Have all handouts copied in advance and at your fingertips.

Give your students specific directions for what to do when they get their papers (turn it facedown on the desk, put name and date on it, immediately begin to complete it, and so on).

Tell students your procedure for collecting papers. Do you want them to pass the papers down a row? Do you want a team captain to collect them for the team? Having all students put the headings (name and date) facing upward in the stack will save you time in rearranging the papers before grading them.

Assign each student a number, based on the alphabetical order of his or her names, to place in the top right corner of each paper. This will allow a student helper to put the papers in order for you. Ask student helpers to give you a list of any missing numbers, and you will know immediately which papers were not turned in. This will also save you time when you grade the papers, as you can easily record the grades in order as you go down the list in your grade book.

Decide on a system for collecting homework. Do you want students to keep it at their desks until you begin that subject? Will you have a homework basket in which students should place their work as they enter in the morning?

Decide on a procedure, consistently enforce it, and students will know what you expect!

10 Have a System for Recording Homework

For younger students, many teachers prepare a weekly homework assignment sheet in advance and give it to each student on Monday. Students often have a homework folder. The assignment sheet and any worksheets or notes go home in the folder, and completed homework is placed in the folder and brought back to school.

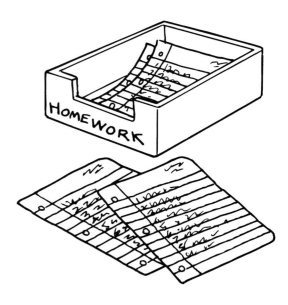

As students get older, they are expected to record their homework each day, perhaps on a homework sheet or in a notebook. Will your students copy their homework at the end of each lesson, or will they copy all of it at the end of the day? If students must copy their assignments at the end of the day, be sure to leave enough time.

Many teachers ask parents to sign students' homework assignment sheets each evening. This way, you will know that parents are aware of the assigned work.

11 Be Sure That Your Students Know Your Expectations about Completing Work When They Are Absent

Do students need to complete all missed classwork and homework? How long do they have to complete the missed work? How will they know what was missed?

Some teachers have folders marked for each day of the week and insert any daily worksheets or handouts in the appropriate folders for absent students. Other teachers assign partners in the classroom. If a student is absent, his partner collects any worksheets and fills him in on the missed work when he returns to class.

Some teachers keep a laminated chart on the classroom wall with the heading HOMEWORK and sections for Monday, Tuesday, Wednesday, Thursday, and Friday. In erasable marker, the teacher records each day's homework on the chart. Absent students are expected to copy down the assignments they missed. Still other teachers have a "homework recorder" as a class job. The recorder writes down the date and homework assignments in a class log, and absent students are expected to copy their assignments from the log.

12 Begin a File

Set up a file drawer with blank folders. As you go through the year, file everything!

When planning a field trip, file the permission slip, the letter to parents, and the site information. Keep a file for curriculum units, bulletin board ideas, center ideas, and newsletters. You will be thrilled next year when you can go to your files and pull out a ready-to-use idea!

13 Keep Up with the Paperwork

Check your mailbox often. You may have an important phone message from a parent, a note from your principal, or papers that need to be sent home as soon as possible.

Handle a paper only once. File it, respond to it, or pass it on. Don't let things sit on your desk, or they could get buried underneath other papers.

Grade your papers, complete your plans, order your supplies, and write your progress reports as they come up. These jobs will only multiply if you procrastinate!

Tips from Teachers. . .

On Rules

"We write rules together. I let students suggest rules, but I guide them. I have a vision of what the final rules should be and the rules my class writes are always very close to that vision."

"When new students enter the classroom in the middle of the year, we review rules and procedures. I let my students explain our rules to the new student. That helps to reinforce them for everyone."

"I read *Lilly's Purple Plastic Purse* by Kevin Henkes to my second graders, and then we discussed Lilly's behavior and the consequences of her behavior."

On Procedures

"Have a fun and easy warm-up ready for students as they enter on the first day. Have them sit down immediately and begin. When everyone has arrived, go over how you want them to enter the classroom each day and then let them put away backpacks and other supplies as you tell them how it should be done."

"I label baskets in my room for items that are being collected (for example, homework, book reports, notes to the teacher, and absentee work). Students are responsible for getting their papers into the right baskets, which means I don't have to sort all of the papers before I begin checking them in or grading them."

"After we've finished discussing the class rules, I have them write our rules in their own words or draw cartoons showing the rules. That helps me see if they understand them."

"At the beginning of the year, we acted out different situations and talked about how they could be handled."

"I begin a positive incentive program on the first day. I make it very visual—like stars on a bulletin board. Then, I give a star every time the class is following the rules we've discussed. This gives me a chance to reinforce the behavior I expect throughout the first week. I try to work it so the class earns a treat by Friday! My treat is a class art project."

"I spend a lot of time during the first few weeks making sure everyone knows our class procedures—how to line up, walk down the hallways, sharpen pencils, hand in papers, turn in homework, and so on. I remind them of the procedures repeatedly and make sure that I am consistent in enforcing them."

"When I walk students down the halls, I have stopping points so that I can monitor their behavior. I teach them where to stop, so the trip from our classroom to the cafeteria is done in 3 stages. Whenever we turn a corner, I stand right at the intersection where I can see both parts of my line."

"If a child walks up to me to ask a question, I just send him or her back to his or her seat to raise his or her hand for permission to get up. The children get the message quickly!"

On Procedures (continued)

"I have a team folder on each table. Teams place completed work in their folders, and then team captains bring their folders to me. It eliminates all of the paper-passing problems."

"My *Sorry You Were Absent* bulletin board has helped me manage absentee work. I put a large manila envelope on the board for each day of the week and place worksheets that were handed out that day in the correct envelop. When a student misses a day, he or she checks the folders for his or her work."

On Beginning the Day

"I greet students at my classroom door with my clipboard. I take attendance as I welcome them to the class."

"I simply scan the room after students are seated, doing their morning warm-up, and take attendance by seeing which desks are empty."

"All students enter the room, unpack backpacks, and begin their morning work. One team at a time sharpens pencils, puts homework in a basket, and hangs up their coats and book bags. Only one team is out of their seats at a time."

"A warm-up activity is on their desks or on the blackboard as students enter. They put their homework and any notes to me on the left corners of their desks. As they work, I move around and collect the papers."

"Students sit in teams. I use a team challenge, where teams earn points for getting settled and starting on their warm-up."

"I teach students a procedure for passing in papers. They may not pass their papers until they have the papers from the students before them. The papers are passed in stacks, not haphazardly."

"Before I collect the homework, I have students place it in the centers of their desks. I quickly look around the room and make note of the empty desks. Then I ask students to pass in their work. This way, I know which papers are missing and can talk to those students without going through the whole stack of papers."

"I do lunch count and attendance with my first graders as a part of my calendar math activities. We tally totals together."

"Students have magnets with their names on them. All of the magnets are in a section of the board marked absent as the day begins. Students then move their magnet to the buying lunch or brought lunch sections on my board. I can take attendance and lunch count just by glancing at the magnets."

"I have a numbered list on a clipboard each morning. My fifth grade students sign the list if they are buying lunch. I quickly read off the list before I send my count to the cafeteria. My team captains tally the lunch counts for their teams."

"Students check the overhead as they enter the room. The items they need to keep at their desks are written on it. They also get directions for an Early Bird assignment."

Tips from Teachers. . .

On Ending the Day

"I go over homework, and we write it together on the homework charts. Since the charts are in their take-home folders, it's a good time to pass out graded papers. Then they file their graded papers and any newsletters that are going home in their folders."

"We write daily news together at the end of the day. The children give me sentences about their day. I begin the next day by reading their sentences."

"I have students pack up everything except their library books; then they read until it's time for afternoon announcements."

"Teams are silently dismissed to get their coats and backpacks. I do this by silently holding up each team number. Since I don't call out the number, they need to be watching me. And they know I won't hold up their number if their team is not quiet and ready!"

"Everyone likes to help wash the boards, so I pick afternoon helpers who are getting ready quietly. They all try to be my helper, and it keeps our cleanup quiet."

"The p.a. system doesn't dismiss my students, I do. Buses are called in groups over the p.a. system, but my students know to stay in their seats until I call each bus, one at a time, after the announcements are over."

"During cleanup time, I ask students questions about math or social studies lessons we've done that day. It helps us wrap up the day and keeps everyone focused on me and quiet during cleanup."

"On the blackboard, we make a list of all the things that should be in their book bags to go home that day."

"First we pack up our things to go home; then while we're waiting for afternoon announcements, I read a story to the class."

"The buses in our school are designated by colors (the red bus, the blue bus, and so on). I have a laminated bus chart with all of the bus colors listed on it. As buses are called, I check off each color that has been called with an erasable marker. Students can see which buses are here, and I don't have the problem of students missing their buses because they didn't hear the colors that were called."

"The coat hooks in my room are very close together, and students' coats and backpacks frequently ended up on the floor by the end of the day. There was always confusion when it was time to pack up for home. I bought six large plastic bins, each a different color, and had students put their backpacks in the bins that matched their team colors. At the end of the day, a helper brings the correct bin to each team, and students get their backpacks and begin packing for home without confusion."

KEYS TO
Organizing Your Classroom
with Clear Rules
and Procedures

Use the checklist below to see if your class passes the "organized for success" test.

- Our classroom rules are posted in the classroom.

- My students understand and can explain our classroom rules.

- I take the time to notice student behaviors, both appropriate and inappropriate, and comment on them.

- I have procedures in place for all of our daily classroom tasks.

- I reteach procedures when I see that students are having trouble following them.

- Students know how I expect them to enter the classroom each day.

- Students know how to pack up their belongings and get ready to go home in a calm and organized way.

- I am organized in completing my own paperwork.

Classroom Procedures for Room _____

Think about each of the following daily classroom tasks. Jot down the procedure that you've decided on for your classroom. Teach these procedures to your students. Consistently reinforce them. Put a copy of this sheet in your substitute folder.

1. Entering the classroom in the morning

2. Sharpening pencils

3. Permission to use the restroom

4. Getting drinks of water

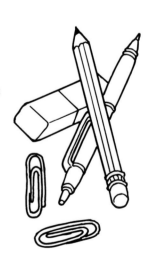

5. Walking in the hallways

7. Entering the classroom from art, P. E., music, lunch, or recess

8. Passing out papers or supplies

9. Handing in papers (classwork and homework)

10. Completing absentee work

11. Participation in learning centers

12. Ending the day (packing to go home)

Chapter 4
Managing Student Behavior

Maintaining good behavior in your classroom requires both rewards and consequences. Students need to be praised when they are behaving appropriately and receive a consequence when their actions are inappropriate.

1 Catch Them Being Good

Notice your students' good behavior and praise them for it! Mention the good behaviors you see, whenever possible. It will encourage others in your class to imitate these behaviors. Make an attempt to praise every child each day. You will create a positive and supportive climate within your classroom.

2 Rewarding Appropriate Behavior

Positive incentives can help maintain appropriate behavior and change inappropriate behavior. Rewards for individual students, as well as small group or class incentives, help manage classroom behavior.

Praise is a very effective reward. Often praise alone is enough to maintain good behavior, especially when it reminds every student in your room of your expectations. For example, "I am so happy with the way you walked down the hall. I didn't hear a sound. I know the classes we passed appreciated how quiet we were."

Small group and class goals may also help to maintain appropriate behavior. You might use a point system. "When the class reaches 50 points, we'll have 15 minutes of extra recess." You might have a jar to fill with marbles; "When the jar is full we'll celebrate with a

popcorn party." Activities like these, which break up the usual routine and celebrate students' successes, will help to enliven your classroom.

Many teachers want students to participate in partner or group activities on a daily basis, so they arrange the desks in their classroom into groups or teams. When students sit in teams, maintaining good classroom behavior

by focusing on team rewards can be very effective. Small group behavior can be monitored with a bingo card for each group. Groups earn treats when they fill their cards with stickers or stars. Team contests allow students to visualize their teams' progress. It is important that students know which behaviors will earn points for their team. The more frequently a teacher catches good behavior, the more on-task the class will stay.

3 Share Positive Messages with Parents!

Have a stack of positive notecards ready to send home. Be specific and tell parents about a positive thing their child did, such as a good grade on a test, helping another student, or a well-written book report. Your students will be thrilled that you let their parents know about their successes.

4 Ideas for Student Rewards

Rewards can be very simple. Effective rewards don't have to cost a lot of money. Here are some ideas for classroom rewards:

Smile

Praise

Stickers/stars/happy faces

Extra computer time

Paperback books

Chance to check out an extra book from the class library

Name displayed on a special bulletin board

Teacher's helper for the day

Award certificates

No homework pass

Line leader

Coloring sheets/word searches

Special seat in class

Positive note home

Daily prize drawings

Read a book to a younger child

Lunch with the teacher

Extra recess

5 When Students Misbehave

When misbehavior does occur, it is important to act on it immediately, consistently, and in a way that does not magnify the problem or distract other students from their lesson. Maximizing time on task is critical for ensuring student achievement in your classroom. Ask yourself a few questions to help you decide the best way to deal with misbehavior.

- *Can I use a simple management technique to control this behavior?*

  Try one of these:

  Move closer to the student

  Call the student's name.

  Compliment another student for appropriate behavior.

  Stop teaching for a moment to get the student's attention.

  Use a silent signal to get the student's attention.

- *Is this a simple behavior that I can modify or correct with a simple consequence?*

  A student pushes to be first in line. Move her to the back of the line.

  A student is playing with his ruler. Take the ruler away.

  A student scribbles on his math paper. Have him recopy it.

  Don't let simple behaviors escalate with long lectures or unreasonable punishments.

- *Do I need to speak with the student about this misbehavior?*

  Try firmly stating what you want the student to be doing. "You need to open your math book and get started on your work."

  Tell the student what you expect his or her behavior to be. "I need you to be sitting in your chair with both feet on the floor."

  Do not get into a debate with a student. Don't take class time to discuss who did what to whom or who is at fault. Set up a time to speak to the student when there is no audience (your class).

- *Does this behavior require a more serious consequence?*

  Change the student's seat.

  Take away a privilege (being class helper, part of recess).

  Have the student make up the missed class time during his or her recess or after school.

  Send the student to a time-out chair in your classroom.

  Send the student to a time-out chair in a colleague's classroom.

  Have the student reflect on his behavior in writing (what he or she did and what he or she will do next time).

  Send a note home to parents, (or call them) alerting them of the behavior.

- *Is this a severe or recurrent behavior that needs to be dealt with in a more serious manner?*

  Schedule a parent conference.

  Speak with the child, parent, and/or administrator about the problem. Initiate some actions to solve the problem.

  Establish a behavior contract with the student and parent.

  Refer the child to a school team that deals with severe or recurrent behavior problems.

Tips from Teachers. . .

On Rewards

"I give students tickets for good behavior. We have an auction at the end of each month, and students use their tickets to buy items."

"As I catch students being good, I give them tickets. They place their names on the tickets and put them in a jar in my room. At the end of each day, I have a drawing and pick out a few tickets for treats."

"I take a picture of a couple students who have been displaying good behavior. The pictures are displayed on the board for a week. Kids love to see themselves!"

"I pin positive notes on my first graders as they get ready to go home."

"I have a special chair in my classroom. It is painted gold and has stars on it. Each day I select a student, based on his/her behavior, to sit in the chair for the next day."

"I put a happy box on the blackboard (a happy face in a square large enough to add some names). As I catch students who are on task, I write their names in the box. It gets everyone's attention, and they all get back on task."

"I keep a jar on my desk, and each time the class earns a reward, I scoop some popcorn into the jar. When the jar is full, we pop the popcorn and have a party."

"I have a Star Student chart in my room. Students like having their names on the chart."

"I make positive phone calls home—just a quick call to tell parents about something positive! It is amazing how happy parents are to get these calls."

"I have a Team of the Week. That team gets to be first to line up, first to get materials, and so on."

"I put a *Good Citizen* certificate on the board with a clip magnet. I make a big deal when someone does something nice, and I fill out his or her name on the certificate and give it to him or her right away!"

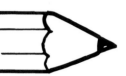

Tips from Teachers. . .

On Consequences

"I call parents immediately whenever there is a problem."

"I send home a weekly parent letter with grades for behavior and work habits."

"I seat the disruptive student close to where I am teaching so that I can monitor him or her closely."

"I take away a privilege; for example, part of recess, use of a center, or a class job."

"When a student continues to break rules, I put together a behavior contract that is sent home daily. I have a parent conference to discuss and set up the contract so parents have input into the rewards and consequences. I always include the child in the conference."

"I have private talks with students during their recess. I ask them to tell me what they have been doing to disrupt the class. We talk about how we can prevent their disruptive behavior."

"I have an empty desk in my room for time-out. The child signals to me when he or she thinks he or she can return to his or her group. If the student disrupts again, he or she goes back to the time-out chair, but this time I tell him or her when he or she can return to the group."

"I pair up with another teacher across the hall and send any disruptive students to her for a 5 or 10 minute time out. When they return to my room, they have to tell me how they are going to improve their behavior."

KEYS TO
Managing Student Behavior

Use the checklist below to see if you are tuned in to students' behavior.

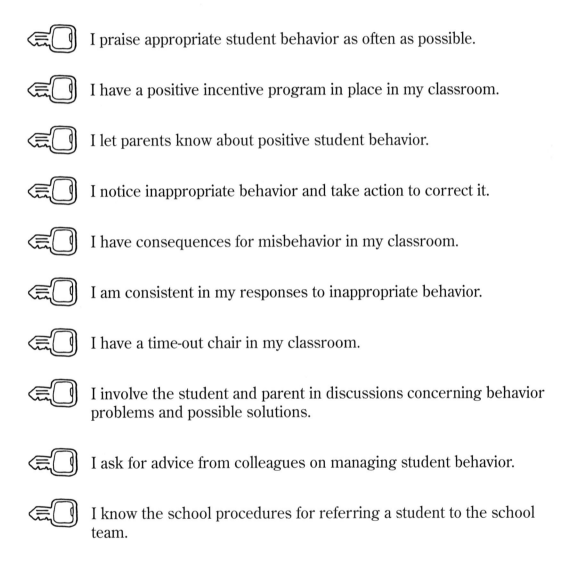

I praise appropriate student behavior as often as possible.

I have a positive incentive program in place in my classroom.

I let parents know about positive student behavior.

I notice inappropriate behavior and take action to correct it.

I have consequences for misbehavior in my classroom.

I am consistent in my responses to inappropriate behavior.

I have a time-out chair in my classroom.

I involve the student and parent in discussions concerning behavior problems and possible solutions.

I ask for advice from colleagues on managing student behavior.

I know the school procedures for referring a student to the school team.

Daily Behavior Contract

Name _____   Date _____

Morning

I completed my work.	Yes	No
I worked quietly.	Yes	No

Afternoon

I completed my work.	Yes	No
I worked quietly.	Yes	No

Homework

I turned in my homework.	Yes	No

Comments:

_____   _____
Parent signature   Teacher signature

Chapter 5
Developing Relations with Students, Staff, and Parents

Staff

1 Get to Know the Staff in Your Building

You don't need to do it all alone! The teachers in your building will be your greatest source of support and assistance. Get to know them as soon as possible. They can assist you in finding appropriate school or community resources. They can answer your questions about school policies and procedures. They can help you plan and can provide you with activity ideas that fit your curriculum.

Keep your door open to your colleagues. Listen to their experience. Trust their tips and strategies. As you feel more comfortable, you can begin to adapt their ideas or strike out on your own.

Volunteer for a school committee—it's a great way to get to know others. The extra time spent on committee work will be rewarded with new staff relationships.

Nearly every staff has some negative people. Recognize who those people are and distance yourself from them. Negativism is contagious. Don't get pulled into negative talk. Keep a positive outlook. If you look for the best in people and situations, you will find them!

The school custodians, secretaries, cafeteria workers, and other staff have a great deal of knowledge to share about the building, school procedures, necessary paperwork, location of supplies, and many other things. Their information will make your year go more smoothly. Introduce yourself!

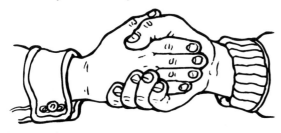

2 Find a Mentor

It is important that you have someone to go to when you have questions or need assistance. Some schools or districts assign mentor teachers to all new teachers. In other schools, mentors are not assigned, but such relationships often develop naturally. If you have not been assigned a mentor, find one within your school. It should be someone with several years' experience. Someone who teaches the same grade level as you would be perfect, but the most important factors should be the comfort you feel in talking with him or her and the willingness and enthusiasm that he or she has for helping you. You will know right away when you meet the right person!

Students

3 Get to Know Your Students

Take an interest in your students. Greet them as they enter your room each morning and wish them well as they leave each afternoon. Early in the year, plan some activities in which students can share a little about themselves (see Chapter 2). Find out when students' birthdays are and recognize their special days, even if just with a note or a special wish.

4 Make Your Students Comfortable

In order to be ready to learn, students in your room need to:

- feel safe
- know your expectations and feel as though they can be successful in your room
- feel as though they belong
- feel respected by you and others in your room

Show respect to students by treating them well, and teach your students how to give and receive compliments and how to respect each other. A respectful tone of voice will be a critical way to show respect to your students. Keep your remarks positive.

Parents

5 Get to Know the Parents of Your Students

Make your first parent contact positive! Send welcome notes home in the first week, introducing yourself to parents and telling them a little about your classroom and the year ahead.

During the first weeks of school, find something positive to say about each child. Send a positive note home. "Erica did a wonderful job on today's math test! I can see that she has been studying. Tell her to keep up the great work!" "Joe helped another student today when she dropped her school supplies. I am so impressed by his helpfulness."

Keep parents informed about classroom events through letters, newsletters, or Websites. Let them know when projects are due, about activities in which students have been involved, and about upcoming special events.

Be careful about giving out your home phone number. If you do this, the number of calls you receive may snowball. Provide parents with other ways to get in touch with you, such as a school phone number or an e-mail address.

6 Begin Parent-Teacher Conferences with Positive Remarks

Begin the first parent conference of the year with a firm handshake, an introduction, and a smile. When talking with a parent about his or her child, either face to face or through written comments, always begin with a positive statement. Show the parent, through your choice of words and tone of voice, that you like his or her child and want the best for him or her.

Be prepared for parent conferences. Look over the student's grades and jot down some key points you'd like to share with parents. Have some work samples available to explain your points. Never mention another child's name during your conference. Focus on one child only.

7 Dealing with Problems

When problems occur, set up a parent conference to discuss the situation. Describe the student's behavior in an objective way. Be careful not to use words with a negative context, such as *lazy*.

After describing the behavior that concerns you, involve parents in the solution. You might agree to send home a note each day letting the parents know about the student's progress or you might invite the parent into your classroom to observe. When progress notes are sent home, ask parents to initial the notes and return them to you. Not only does this reassure you that they are following up at home, but it becomes valuable documentation should further problems arise. Ask parents to praise or reward students who are meeting their goals. Perhaps parents will agree to rent a video or provide a trip to the student's favorite fast food restaurant when a goal is reached. Having home and school work together is much more effective than having a teacher work alone to modify a student's behavior.

If a parent becomes angry or threatens you, politely end the conference or call for an administrator. Document all parent communication, such as notes home, phone calls, and e-mails.

Tips from Teachers. . .

On Building Relationships

"I call each home on the first or second day of school. I tell the parents that I am so glad their children are in my room and that I look forward to working with them this year. I tell them that I look forward to seeing them at Back-to-School Night."

"I have a Lunch Bunch once each week. I invite three students to join me for lunch. We talk about their lives and laugh and have fun. I get to know them so well!"

"I have a *Student of the Week* bulletin board. Each student gets a chance to be highlighted for one week. The student brings in pictures of themselves to decorate the board and write paragraphs about themselves to display on the board."

"I send a class newsletter home each week. On Friday morning, the class dictates sentences about what we've done that week. I write them on the blackboard, and they copy them onto the top of a newsletter during group time. The bottom half of the newsletter has information I send home—field trip reminders, book report due dates, and so on."

"I keep a parent communication log in the back of my grade book. I write down the date, note whether the discussion took place in person, by phone, or e-mail, and summarize the discussion."

"If I suspect that a child is not giving notes to his parents, I send one home through the U.S. mail."

"I ask students to have notes signed by parents and returned to me. I keep a file of all returned notes. It has come in handy several times when parents insisted that they were unaware of a problem. I was able to produce the note with their signature."

"When I have a parent conference that results in a student contract, I always send a little note home after a few days to thank the parents for their support."

KEYS TO
Building Relationships

Use the checklist below to see how well you've connected with others.

- I greet my students as they enter the classroom.

- I know something special about each of my students.

- I frequently talk to other teachers at my grade level.

- I have become involved in a school committee to get to know others in the building.

- I know the secretaries, custodians, and other support staff.

- I have a teaching professional who serves as my mentor.

- I ask for help when needed.

- I have introduced myself to parents, either through notes or phone calls home.

- I keep parents informed about classroom activities and their child's progress.

- I have given all parents opportunities to sign up for parent conferences.

- I am prepared for conferences with work samples, grades, and individual comments.

- I begin parent conferences on a positive note.

- When problems occur with children, I involve parents in the solution.

It's Time for Parent Conferences!

Date: _____

Time: _____

Place: _____

I look forward to meeting with you to discuss your child's progress.

Please sign and return the form below to indicate whether you will be able to attend the conference.

_____

Teacher

✂ - ✂

Student's name: _____

I am able to attend the conference scheduled on

_____ at _____.

      (date)   (time)

_____

Parent signature

       reproducible

Chapter 6
Planning, Delivering, and Assessing Instruction

Planning

1 Planning Instruction

Know your curriculum. Take time to review curriculum guides and teacher's editions of textbooks. Understand the objectives that you are striving to meet. Does your state have a particular set of standards or outcomes that will guide your instruction? Does your school or school district have a specific curriculum that you must follow?

Planning is your key to success. A combination of long-range and short-range planning will guide your instruction throughout the year.

2 Long-Range Plans

You will need a long-range plan to move at a pace that will allow you to cover the expected curriculum during the coming year. You may use a monthly calendar format for your long-range plans; pencil in units/chapters as you plan to cover them throughout the year. Doing this at the start of the year will help you determine the amount of time you will be able to spend on any particular unit.

3 Short-Range Plans

Your weekly planning should be done in a plan book that allows space for you to jot down the specifics of each lesson. Recording the lesson's objectives, the materials you will use, a description of the lesson's activities, and related assessment activities will provide you with the guidance you need for each day's lessons. Some new teachers even write down questions or statements they will make during the lesson. By thinking through the dialogue of the lesson,

they feel better prepared to conduct it. The more thoroughly you have thought out each lesson, the better prepared you will feel when you deliver it to your students. Do your weekly planning in pencil, as changes will undoubtedly need to be made!

4 Keys to a Well-Developed Lesson

In planning your lessons, remember to include the following:

- Warm-up activities to focus the students on the topic or to review prior knowledge or prerequisite skills that may be necessary for the success of the lesson

- Statement of objectives so that everyone is clear about what the endpoint should be

- Demonstration/explanation/modeling of the skill or concept

- Guided practice for students, during which you provide students with appropriate feedback

- Independent practice to allow students to try it on their own

- Assessment to be sure that students understood the lesson and met the objective
- Closure activities to summarize what has been learned and bring closure to the lesson

5 Preparing for the Day's Lessons

Read your lesson plans the night before.

Put your lesson plans on your desk.

Gather the materials you will need, including student materials (worksheets, manipulatives) and teacher materials (overhead transparencies, teacher's editions). Have them in an easily accessible spot before students arrive for the day.

Prepare any chart paper or sentence strips in advance.

Plan for a variety of different learning styles (auditory, visual, kinesthetic).

6 Know Where to Find Resources

Ask other teachers. Become familiar with storage/book rooms. Look through supplemental materials in the teacher's guides. Become familiar with what is in your school.

Be sure that the materials and resources you use are culturally diverse. Students should see their cultures represented in your classroom materials and should become introduced to other cultures as well. And be sure that all reading materials are at the correct readability levels for your students. Providing books or written tasks that are too difficult will result in a great deal of anxiety and frustration for your students.

If you plan to use equipment to present lessons, be sure to check if it is available at your school. Is each classroom suitably equipped to allow you to use technology as a teaching tool? Will you need to sign out equipment from a central location? How far in advance will you need to reserve the equipment? Always set up equipment well before your lesson and try it out to be sure there that are no technical difficulties.

Delivering Instruction

7 Know the Material/Content

Review your lesson plans the night before a lesson. Be certain to read all student worksheets and textbook chapters. You may want to carry a clipboard holding your lesson plan if it helps you feel more comfortable when delivering your lessons. Soon you will relax and may not that need extra support.

8 Give Clear Directions

Be sure to break down the directions into small steps. Do students need to read the chapter first? Will they need to gather materials? How should they record the information? Provide a clear sequence to the activities to clarify the task for students. After you have given directions, ask students to repeat them for you. Do they know what to do? If they seem unclear, explain the directions again.

9 Watch and Listen to Your Students

Teaching requires interaction. Listen to your students' responses and questions. By listening to them, you will know what they have heard. Don't continue with your lesson if students' comments tell you that you should restate, modify, or clarify.

10 Differentiate Your Instruction

Modify your assignments to meet the needs of different students. All students do not have to do the same assignment. Challenge those who can do more by adding extra problems to their worksheet; reduce the number of problems on assignments for students who are having difficulty.

Don't be afraid to form groups for reteaching. There will often be students who do not understand lessons. Pulling these students together for ten-minute reteaching lessons while the rest of the class works on independent practice activities, may be all it takes to help them become successful.

Centers not only allow you to provide review for students who are having difficulty but also challenge students who are able to move at a quicker pace. You might provide a library area, a computer area, a writing center with topic ideas, or a math center with real-world activities in which students apply classroom skills.

If you have difficulty modifying classroom lessons and activities for students who are working below grade level, talk to the special education teacher. He or she will have lots of ideas to share with you.

Good teaching is not about giving every child the same instruction; it is about giving every child the instruction that he or she needs to be successful.

11 Involve All Students in Your Lesson

Call on all students. Be careful not to call only on energetic hand-raisers. Many teachers use equity cards—index cards with students' names—so that they can draw cards and call on students in random order. This provides equality in calling on students and keeps students guessing about who might be called next.

Move around the room to monitor students' work and to keep students involved in your lesson. Have more than one instructional area in your classroom so that you can vary where you stand (maybe a blackboard in one part of the room and some chart paper in another). Wear comfortable shoes; you will be doing a lot of walking!

12 Make Your Lessons Motivating

Remember that students have different learning styles. Have you included opportunities for students to gain information through hands-on exploration, visual displays, and discussion? Have you included technology in your presentations?

Be careful not to lecture to students for extended time periods. If you have content to deliver, can it be delivered in a more interactive way? Can you mix in opportunities for students to discuss a topic, predict an answer, or brainstorm ideas? Keep your students involved in your lessons!

13 Provide Students with Opportunities to Learn from Each Other

Having students work in groups requires preplanning and careful classroom management. Be sure to consider the behavior and academic abilities of your students before creating your teams. Talk to your students about what you expect from them during group work. The following are critical to the success of group activities:

- Give clear directions before asking students to begin a group task. Check to see that all groups understand the task.

- Assign a role/responsibility to each group member. Be sure that everyone understands his or her role. Typical roles might include reader, leader, recorder, reporter, supplies manager, and timekeeper. Choose the roles that will help the group complete the assigned task.

- Teach students a "quiet" signal before beginning any group activity. The signal might be counting down from 5 to 1, holding up a hand, or flickering a light, and it indicates to everyone that you have something to say and that the room should be silent. Practice the signal with your students, praising them for quick response.

- Following group work, assess students independently to be sure that each of them learned the necessary skill.

14 Bring Closure to Your Lessons

Before ending any lesson, review what was learned. Summarize the lesson for students or ask them to summarize it for you. Ask them to tell you something they learned and decide whether they achieved the lesson objective. Talk about what you will be doing tomorrow.

Assessment and Evaluation

15 Assess Students Frequently and in a Variety of Ways

Your goal is success for all of your students. It is your job to monitor and adjust your instruction so that success is possible for all.

Assessment should be ongoing in your classroom. Watch and listen to your students. Ask questions frequently.

Many forms of all-pupil response will allow you to check the comprehension of the whole class. You might ask for a thumbs-up or thumbs-down response to a question. Pinch cards (index cards with the same responses on both sides) are popular with many teachers, as they allow a teacher to quickly scan a room for student responses. When using pinch cards, students are asked to pinch their responses to a question. Pinch cards might show a happy face and sad face or contain the words *yes/no, true/false,* or *right/wrong.* The teacher poses questions, and students pinch their responses to each.

Observing students at work is very important. Did students take too long to complete a task? Did they breeze through it quickly?

Did they appear frustrated? Are there flaws in the method they are using? Many teachers move around the room with clipboards, making notes as they observe students or marking checklists that indicate students' strengths and weaknesses.

Traditional paper-and-pencil tests provide information on students' skills. There are many formats for tests—multiple choice, true or false, fill-in-the-blank, analogy, and open-ended. Using a variety of formats will provide you with a wealth of information.

The use of open-ended tests (student written responses) will be especially helpful in assessing critical thinking, as you may ask students to explain and justify answers. Getting a glimpse into students' thinking will better allow you to modify your instruction to meet their needs.

Portfolios compile student work and demonstrate their progress. In some portfolios, the teacher specifies the work samples that should be included. In others, students are given permission to include self-selected "best work" samples. In order to make portfolios more than just collections of student work samples, it is important to include students' reflections on their work. Allow students to review their portfolio work and comment on what they have done well and what might need improvement.

17 Provide Students with Timely and Specific Feedback on Their Work

Students deserve feedback on assignments. This does not mean that you have to grade each paper. Decide on whether a paper needs to be graded or reviewed with the class. For some activities, reviewing answers and having a class discussion may be appropriate. For others, you will want to see each paper and provide a grade and comments that help the child understand the grade.

Be timely in your feedback to students. Grading papers and providing feedback is meant to guide your students in their learning and you in your teaching. If you are two weeks behind in getting feedback to students, the feedback may no longer be important; as

the class may have moved beyond those skills. Discovering, and then addressing, misunderstandings or errors in students' work must be done in a timely manner so that students do not practice skills incorrectly.

Be kind when you mark on students' papers. It can be humiliating for students to get their work back with big red marks all over it! If it appears that the student has completely misunderstood, put the paper aside and come up with a plan to help the student become successful. Do you have time to reteach the skill to this student or to a small group who didn't understand? Could a student in your room serve as a peer tutor? Could you involve the parent in home support? Is there a resource teacher or aide at your school who could be of assistance?

Don't get frustrated with students when you see several errors in their work. Think back on your lesson. Figure out a way to reteach it, focusing on weak areas. If you see many errors, your lesson may not have been clear. Don't blame; just reteach.

If a student in your class has repeated difficulty with lessons and assignments, look in his or her official school records to see if they have any information of which you should be aware, such as past history, medical condition, or previous assessments. Every school has a team that discusses academic or behavior concerns. Find out how to refer a student to this team. Before referring the student, however, be sure that you have tried intervention in your classroom. Have you moved his or her seat closer to the instructional area? Have you modified the work? Have you talked with the parent? Write down any interventions that you have tried, so that you can report them to the school team. This team may be able to provide you with additional suggestions to help the child succeed.

18 Evaluate Student Progress on Report Cards and Progress Notes

Evaluating students is the process of combining all of the assessment information you have gathered (including items such as test grades, observations, work samples, and discussions) and then assigning grades to report their progress. Before beginning the school year, look at your school's report cards and progress reports so that you are familiar with the way in which you will be asked to evaluate your students. Which areas are to be evaluated? Reading? Math? Work habits? Behavior? Will you be asked to provide a percentage? Letter grades? Commentary? What types of comments are asked for on the report? Once you are familiar with the report card, organize your grade book according to what you will be expected to evaluate.

A report card generally has a comments section. In writing your comments, try to say something positive, mention something that needs improvement, and suggest a way that parents might help at home.

In most schools, progress reports are sent home midway through a grading period if a student's performance is less than satisfactory. Be as specific as possible on these reports. Offer ways to parents to help at home. And offer opportunities for parents to speak with you about the reports.

19 Reflect on Lessons That Do Not Go Well

If things don't go as planned, use it as a learning experience. Think about your lesson and analyze what went wrong (see *Help! My Lesson Didn't Go Well* on page 53).

Go back and try the lesson again from a different angle. Don't just redo the lesson as before. If you're not sure, consult a teacher's guide, resource book, or a colleague. Don't forget to reflect on activities that go well, too. You may recognize the keys as to why they are successful.

Tips from Teachers. . .

On Planning

"During my first year, I saved all of my lesson plans in a three-ring binder. I put them into sections for reading, math, science, social studies, and so on. It was so exciting to pull out completed lesson plans during my second year."

"When I see an idea I like in a teacher resource book, I make a copy of it and file it in my idea files which are arranged by topic. That way I have the idea right where I need it when I am planning lessons."

"I always start my planning by listing the objective and then deciding on an assessment that will show if the students met the objective. That way, as I write the rest of my lesson plan, I am always thinking about what I will need to do to be sure that students are successful on the lesson assessment."

"I always use a pencil when writing in my plan book."

"I keep a copy of my long-range plans posted near my desk so I can frequently check to see if we are moving at an appropriate pace."

"Our grade level teams plan together. We get together one afternoon each week and plan lessons for the following week. We talk about lesson ideas and resources. The lessons look different in each classroom because we add our own touches to them, but we have the advantage of planning and sharing as a group."

Tips from Teachers. . .

On Cooperative Learning

"I use colored dots to color code each desk: red, yellow, blue, green. Before each activity, I post a chart, which lists a color and the job that matches. Each student knows his or her job by looking at the color of the dot on his or her desk."

"Before I start an activity, I talk with students about the noise level and behavior I expect. After the lesson, we go back to the chart and evaluate."

"I praise groups frequently on their noise level, productivity level, and so on."

"I raise my hand when I need everyone to be quiet. As students see my hand up, they stop working and raise their hands. When all hands are up and it is silent, I share what I need to say."

"Each month I hang something above each group's table. (October = pumpkins; November =turkeys.) The table that shows good cooperation gets rewarded with seeds on their pumpkin or feathers on their turkey. The table with the most at the end of the month eats lunch with me."

"I always take time at the end of a group activity to praise groups for specific behaviors that were outstanding (for example, the red group for the way they calmly solved a problem and compromised on their solution; the blue group for the way they cleaned up their area). I try to be very specific so all of the students know the behaviors that I value."

"I put all materials in group baskets. That way, the group leader picks up the basket, and the group has everything they need for the task."

KEYS TO
Designing Your Classroom

Use the checklist below to see if you have thoroughly planned for your day's lessons.

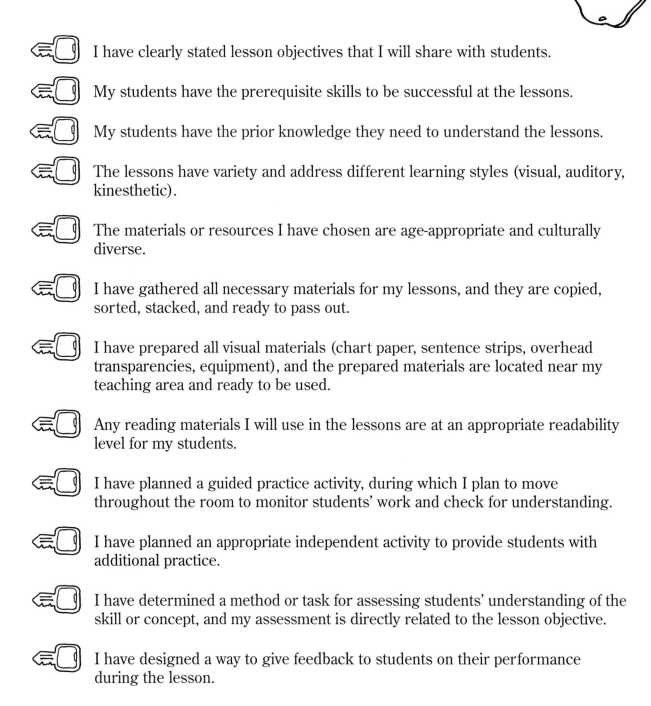

I have clearly stated lesson objectives that I will share with students.

My students have the prerequisite skills to be successful at the lessons.

My students have the prior knowledge they need to understand the lessons.

The lessons have variety and address different learning styles (visual, auditory, kinesthetic).

The materials or resources I have chosen are age-appropriate and culturally diverse.

I have gathered all necessary materials for my lessons, and they are copied, sorted, stacked, and ready to pass out.

I have prepared all visual materials (chart paper, sentence strips, overhead transparencies, equipment), and the prepared materials are located near my teaching area and ready to be used.

Any reading materials I will use in the lessons are at an appropriate readability level for my students.

I have planned a guided practice activity, during which I plan to move throughout the room to monitor students' work and check for understanding.

I have planned an appropriate independent activity to provide students with additional practice.

I have determined a method or task for assessing students' understanding of the skill or concept, and my assessment is directly related to the lesson objective.

I have designed a way to give feedback to students on their performance during the lesson.

Help! My Lesson Didn't Go Well

Did students have the prerequisite skills and prior knowledge that they needed?

When did the lesson start going off track?

Were the directions clear? Did I use understandable vocabulary and include all steps in the directions?

Did I model/demonstrate effectively?

How can I explain or model the skill differently?

Did students have enough time to practice with my assistance?

Some ideas for reteaching this lesson:

Chapter 7
Special and Unexpected Events

Field Trips

Field trips are exciting events for elementary students. They give you the opportunity to bring your lessons to life!

1 Check with the Office Regarding Field Trip Procedures in Your School

Do grade levels plan trips together, or does each classroom teacher plan his/her own?

Do teachers request buses?

How much will a bus cost?

How far in advance must your field trip be scheduled?

Does it get posted on a school calendar?

Is there a schoolwide permission form, or do teachers create their own?

How should money be recorded, and when should it be sent to the office?

Several weeks prior to your trip, send a note home to parents with information about the trip (where, when, why, cost, dress), including a permission form. Keep track of all permission slips that are returned, and send reminders home with students who forget to return them.

Ask for parent chaperones to help you on your trip. Give them specific responsibilities. You may assign a small group of students to each chaperone. If the whole class stays together, you may ask a chaperone to lead the line or be last in line to prevent stragglers. You may ask a chaperone to take care of lunch bags and distribute them to students at the appropriate time. However you choose to delegate responsibilities, share your plan with your chaperones. Be sure that each chaperone knows the rules and procedures for the trip. Can students get out of their seats on the bus? Can students change groups if they want to?

Can students buy souvenirs? Meeting with the parent chaperones prior to the trip or having a list of the procedures for the trip will help ensure that everything runs smoothly.

2 Share Your Behavior Expectations with Students

Discuss appropriate bus behavior, giving specific examples so that all students understand. Discuss the behaviors you expect at the site and share specific procedures with students. Will they be assigned to a chaperone, or will the class stay together as a whole? Will they carry their lunches with them, or will lunches be distributed to everyone on site? Will they be allowed to buy sodas or other snacks, or should they pack all of their own food? Are they allowed to bring books, pencils, or any other objects? Things will go more smoothly if everyone knows what you expect.

3 Make Your Trip an Educational Experience

Before going on the field trip, talk about the site. Prepare students for their visit with some background knowledge. You may want to ask students pre-trip questions in order to guide their observations.

When you return to school, discuss the trip with students. Connect the trip to what students are learning in school. Plan a post-trip activity such as writing a summary of the day, writing a thank-you letter to someone who helped on the trip, drawing a picture of something seen, or writing a letter to parents to tell them about the trip.

Assemblies

Assemblies provide a break from the daily routine in the school and offer students a wide variety of artistic, educational, and cultural experiences.

4 Be Sure That You Know the Assembly Procedures in Your School

Are students called on the p.a. system when it is time to come to the assembly, or do you just bring your class at a certain time? Where do teachers sit during the assembly? Are classes dismissed one at a time?

Think about student seating as you line students up to go to the assembly. Are there students who should not sit together? Separate them in your line so that they do not end up sitting next to each other. Are there students who should sit near the end of aisles where you can see them?

Before going to the assembly, tell students what you expect of their behavior. Are they to be quiet during the assembly? Should they wait for you to let them know when to line up after the assembly?

Remind your students to use the bathroom before the assembly.

Be aware of the assembly topic and objective. Focus students on the topic with some pre-assembly discussions and follow up with discussions or a post-assembly writing activity.

5 Praise Positive Student Behaviors after the Assembly

After each assembly, give students feedback on their behavior. Let them know that you appreciate their polite and appropriate behavior.

Parent Visitations

There are usually several days during the school year when parents are invited to visit the school. Back-to-School Night occurs early in the year and is usually an evening program for teachers to welcome parents and explain the curriculum. Later in the year, many schools have a Parent Visitation Day or Open House during the regular school day, when parents are invited to drop in on the class. Both days provide a wonderful opportunity for you to show parents all of the wonderful things you are doing with their children.

6 Plan Carefully for Your Back-to-School Night Presentation

Check with your principal to see if your school has specific issues that you should address. Then prepare a presentation to tell parents about the coming year.

Begin with a welcome. Tell parents how excited you are to be working with their children. Smile and show your enthusiasm. Have all students' work displayed around the room.

Prepare a presentation about your curriculum and your plans for the coming year. If appropriate, use some visuals, such as overhead transparencies or slide shows to make the presentation more interesting. You may want to prepare a handout for parents containing the key points of your presentation.

During your presentation, be sure to mention any upcoming events—assemblies, field trips, or special projects—that are planned for the year. Describe some of the exciting resources you will be using in the classroom, such as computer software, math manipulatives, or science materials. Explain the grading system and let parents know when progress reports will come home. Inform parents of your classroom rules and procedures. Place students' textbooks and copies of their work on students' desks. This is a good time to invite interested parents to sign up for individual conferences as well as to encourage them to become classroom volunteers.

7 Parent Visitation Days Allow Parents to See You Interact with Their Children

Be positive. Have fun. Show the parents that you enjoy what you do!

Parent visitation during the school day can be distracting to students. Understand this; don't get frustrated. Plan simple activities. Don't begin any complex lessons, where student attention is essential. Stay away from lessons in which classroom management may be a problem. You may want to try a few activities in which parents can join their children, such as solving math riddles or shared reading activities.

When parents visit during the school day, have extra chairs in your room, if possible. Make sure that they feel welcome. Have a sign-up sheet as they enter the room. You may not know all of the parents and may want to look over the list at the end of the day to see who entered your room. You may even want to send a short thank-you note to parents who took the time to visit your classroom.

Parties/Indoor Recess

8 Know Your School's Policies for Indoor Celebrations or Recess

Whether it's a special holiday party or just recess on a rainy or cold day, it is important that all students know what is allowed during indoor celebrations. Can students get out of their seats and move around the room? Are there certain games or materials that they can use at this time? Who is responsible for the cleanup?

Some teachers prefer to plan class activities, such as games or movies. Games like hangman, twenty questions, or adaptations of current game shows are popular. Check with your principal about your school policy on showing movies to students. Many schools have approved lists from which movies must be selected.

Some teachers allow students to play board games in small groups. Asking for donations of used games can provide some indoor recess fun, but be sure that you have enough games for all students. And be sure that you provide cleanup time and have a place in your classroom to store games.

Most teachers prefer easy food for parties—cupcakes instead of cakes that must be cut, or boxed drinks instead of jugs that must be poured. Always have plenty of napkins for unexpected spills; have a plan for cleaning up your classroom. Parent volunteers are helpful when food is in your plans!

Observations of Your Teaching

All new teachers are observed by the principal or another school administrator. This can be a very stressful event, but thorough planning is your key to success.

9 Plan a Solid but Simple Lesson

The biggest mistake that new teachers make is trying to do it all in their observation lessons. While you may want to show your principal all of the great things you can do, remember that he or she will see that in time. Don't try to fit it all into one lesson. If the lesson is too long, you are likely to lose your students' attention.

Simple lessons are best. Don't get too fancy. If the lesson is done in a new format, such as a new cooperative learning technique, you may have some unexpected management problems. Don't do anything for the first time during an observation.

Be thoroughly planned. Think through all of the steps of the lesson. Think about what you will say and anticipate mishaps. What will you do if no one volunteers to answer? What if there is an uneven number in a group?

Keep a copy of your lesson plan nearby so that you can look at it if you are nervous. Have all of your materials ready, such as overhead pens, charts, and copies of handouts.

Have a place for the observer to sit. Provide him or her with a copy of your lesson plan and any textbooks, resource books, or handouts you will be using.

All new teachers are nervous about first observations, but remember that observations provide feedback that will help you become a more effective teacher. Plan thoroughly, anticipate problems, listen to your students to be sure that they understand, and then relax and go with your instincts. If you have to repeat a part of the lesson, or if you don't finish everything you had planned, don't panic. You will most likely have a post-observation conference, at which time you can explain your decisions and discuss your instructional strategies.

Dealing with the Unexpected

10 Substitutes

Being a substitute is not an easy job! Do your best to help the day go smoothly for the substitute and for your students.

If your absence is expected, leave a detailed note for your substitute, explaining the tasks you would like him or her to do. Gather any worksheets, supplies, or textbooks that the substitute will need and leave them in a stack on your desk. Always leave a read aloud book on your desk.

You never know when you might be sick, but there are some things you can do to prepare for those emergency absences. Keep a substitute folder with extra activity ideas such as math review, map activity, language arts review, handwriting paper, or writing prompt. Provide a daily schedule with times for lunch, recess, and other daily activities, an attendance list, a list of classroom rules and consequences, a list of classroom procedures, and a sheet for the substitute to provide you with feedback on the day. Be sure to also include a list of any students who leave your classroom for special services during the day. Leave this substitute folder in the school office, with a colleague, or in an obvious place in your classroom so that it can be found if you are unexpectedly absent. And keep your classroom and desk organized so that others can find what they need!

Talk to your students about the behaviors you expect if there is ever a substitute in the room. Let them know that if you are ever absent, you expect awesome behavior for the substitute, and that you will be asking the substitute for the names of the students who are helpful and responsible. Provide students with feedback when you return. Were you proud of the report you received? Were you disappointed? Let them know.

11 Fire Drills

Fire drills are a serious responsibility for all teachers. Check with your office for the specific fire drill procedures in your school; teach these to the children. After talking about what to do, have a fire drill.

Post your fire drill procedures in the classroom. Common procedures include walking silently, closing the classroom door after the last student leaves, following a specified path to a particular exit, lining up in a specific place on the school grounds, and lining up facing away from the school.

Many schools encourage teachers to bring class lists outdoors with them so that they can check attendance when they get outside.

Ask the office for clarification on the procedure if a student or students are out of your room during the fire drill.

After every fire drill, give students feedback on how they did. Be specific about what they did well and what they need to work on.

12 Student Illness/Injury

Know the health history of your students. Do any suffer from asthma or allergies? Do any of your students take medications that you should be aware of? If a student becomes sick in your classroom, he or she is usually sent to the office or health room. Check with your school for specific procedures. If a student is too sick to leave the room, call the office for assistance.

Do not give any medication to students (even aspirin or cough medicine). Check with your school office for the school's policy on giving medicine to students.

If a student is hurt on the playground, send for the school nurse or another adult. Stay calm and move the other children away from the injured student. Always have disposable gloves available for bleeding injuries.

Parents should be notified if students are sick or injured in school. The office or school nurse may contact parents, but check to be sure that someone has notified them.

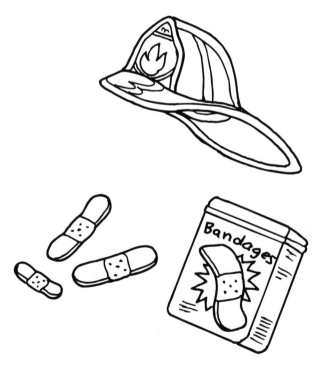

Tips from Teachers. . .

On Special Events

"I ask for two volunteers to be room mothers at the beginning of the year. If I am planning a party or special event, I call the room mothers and let them know what I need (supplies, refreshments, volunteers, and so on), and then they call parents and organize donations or get a list of volunteers. It saves me a lot of time and gets them involved in my class activities."

"I have my students make personal invitations to their parents to visit our class on Open House Day. I have them put our daily schedule in the invitations so parents can plan which subject they might like to see."

"I go to yard sales and buy inexpensive games for indoor recess."

"After field trips, we make a class book about the trip. Each student writes a page about his or her favorite part of the trip, and then we bind the pages together. I put the book in our library area, and students often take it to their seats to read it!"

"I ring a bell when there are three minutes left in indoor recess. The bell signals that it is cleanup time. When I ring the bell again three minutes later, I praise everyone who is at their seats ready to begin the next lesson."

"I put a big welcome sign on our classroom door for our Parent Open House. I put multicolored markers by the sign and ask parents who visit to sign their names on it."

"I play hangman at indoor recess and use spelling or vocabulary words. The students think it's fun, but they are getting a review at the same time."

"I always ask students to tell me something new that they learned after a school assembly. It gives us a chance to talk about the assembly, and it's fun to hear their responses."

KEYS TO
Handling Emergencies

Use the checklist below to see if you are ready for an emergency.

 I have a substitute folder, which contains a variety of instructional activities, a class list, a list of important classroom procedures, and a copy of my daily schedule, in case of my unexpected absence.

 I have spoken to my students about what I expect of their behavior if I am ever absent.

 My room is organized so that a substitute could find appropriate materials.

 I am aware of school fire drill procedures and have explained them to my students.

 I have fire drill procedures posted in my room.

 I know any important medical concerns of my students.

 There are plastic gloves available for the teacher on recess duty.

 I know the procedures for contacting parents if a child is sick or injured at school.

We're Planning a Field Trip

Our class is planning a field trip to _____ on

_____ .

The purpose of our trip is

_____ .

Students will need to bring the following:

_____ .

Please sign the permission slip below and return it to

school by _____ .

Thank you.

_____

------ ✂ -----------------------------------✂ ----------

My child, _____ , has my permission to go on

the field trip to _____ on _____ .

_____
Parent Signature

❏ I would be willing to chaperone. Feel free to contact me.

The best time to get a hold of me is _____ at _____ .

reproducible

Chapter 8
Reflecting On the Joys and Challenges of Teaching

Take Time to Appreciate the Joys of Teaching

Take it slow the first year—you don't have to do it all! When things are frantic, stop and take a deep breath. Appreciate and celebrate your successes!

- Keep a scrapbook.
- Take pictures of things that make you proud.
- Remind yourself of your accomplishments.
- Slow down and take time to notice the children and their smiles.
- Be willing to laugh at yourself.
- Admit your mistakes and correct them.
- Save positive notes from parents and students.
- Read something inspirational when you've had a rough day.

Take time to remind yourself how lucky you are to be a teacher! When you are having a crazy day, take a minute to remember why you chose teaching as a profession. Look at the students and remember what an important role you play in their lives.

1 Recognizing the Challenges of Teaching

Recognize what you have the power to change and strive to change it. You can make a difference in a child's life.

Continue to strive, even when you are not always successful. Know that making a difference often takes time.

Recognize what you do not have the power to change and accept it. Know that you are doing your best and be satisfied with yourself.

2 Reflect on Your Teaching

Take time to think about your successes and failures. Reflect on your experiences. Learn from the painful ones and take pride in the special moments.

- Keep a journal.

  When lessons do not go well, take a few minutes to jot down your thoughts. Think about why; then commit to changing it in your next lesson. When lessons do go well, jot down your thoughts and feelings. Celebrate your successes!

- Videotape yourself teaching and watch yourself.

  Was your lesson well organized? Were your directions clear? Did you call on a variety of students? Do you look relaxed? Are you enjoying the lesson?

Better yet, watch your students on the tape. What are they doing? Are you surprised at what is going on in the class? Are they involved in your lessons?

Don't worry about delivering a "perfect" lesson; just make each lesson a little better than the last one.

- Talk to other teachers in your building.

  Ask if there are any other new teachers who might like to get together for informal meetings. Are you concerned about an area of your teaching that another teacher might be able to help you with? Would a colleague be willing to do a peer observation and give you some tips?

- Problem solve when necessary.

  When you are having a problem with a student or a lesson, think about your options. What might you do? What are the pros and cons of each option? After you have decided, choose a course of action.

3 Become a Dedicated Professional

Join a professional organization, subscribe to a professional journal, attend professional conferences, or browse through professional Web sites. Become involved in your profession and become familiar with the professional resources available to you.

4 Be a Lifelong Learner

Teachers must be lifelong learners. During your career, you will experience teaching different grade levels, working with different groups of students, using a variety of textbooks and teacher resources, working with a myriad of colleagues, and absorbing many new trends in education. There is always something new to experience.

Don't get stuck in your ways. There are more ways than yours to do everything. Be open to new ideas.

Take advantage of professional development opportunities. Stimulate your mind with classes and workshops. Always look for new ideas to enhance your teaching.

5 Stay Focused on Your Students

Teaching is a complex career. You must manage a classroom full of children, differentiate instruction so that all of them can learn, accommodate all of their different learning styles, manage a mountain of paperwork, and communicate with parents about their child's progress. You are a significant person in your students' lives. You nurture them and teach them. You cheer them up when they are feeling down, give them confidence when it is lacking, and open their eyes to new and exciting possibilities for themselves.

Remember that each of your students comes to you from a different place, with unique needs and abilities. You have the power to help each child grow. Do the best you can for each one of them. They will remember you for a lifetime.

Tips from Teachers...

On Enjoying Your Career

"Before I go home each day, I think of something I am proud of doing. Even if it's been a busy day, I go home feeling good."

"I designate one night each week as 'no homework' night for myself. I do my plans before I leave school, and I bring nothing home that night!"

"There was a teacher in my building who was using worksheets she had used for 20 years. She missed so many new and fun activities and seemed bored with every day."

"I try to take a course each year to expand my own skills."

"I organized a book club with other teachers at my school. We get together once a month to discuss a book we've read. It's so nice to read for pleasure and share it with others."

"Whenever there's an evening meeting at school, a group of us goes out to dinner together. It's so nice to talk in a relaxed way."

"I had a student who seemed to always be in trouble. I spent lots of time with her, talking about her behavior and making contracts, which were always broken. I thought of her as one of my failures, until several years later when I got a beautiful letter from her telling me how much I helped her and how well she was doing in middle school."

KEYS TO
Loving Your Career

I remain focused on my students.

I celebrate my successes.

I reflect on my experiences, both positive and negative.

I take time to relax.

I continue to look for new and exciting ideas to use in my classroom.

I continue to learn from others.

I am actively involved in my profession.

I recognize the importance of the job I do.

Chapter 9
Activity Ideas to Get You Started

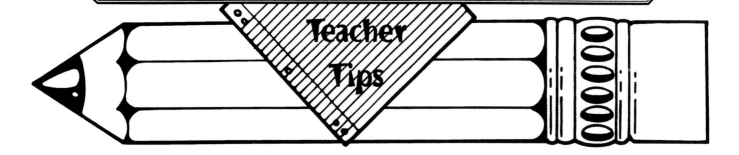

Back-to-School

Teacher Tips

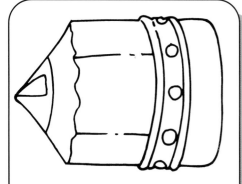

Ask each student to write and illustrate one sentence about: "Something I want to happen this year at school."

Then do your best to make those wishes come true during the year.

Dream up and stitch up a class crest or banner. Give each student a 6" (15 cm) square of burlap, a needle, and yarn. Have each student stitch a design that represents himself or herself. Sew all the squares together.

For your primary class, string up a time line with the names of the months taped or stapled on at 2' (.61 m) intervals. Clip each student's name and birthday in the proper place. Add other holidays and special events throughout the year. Use often for estimating time and so on.

August   September   October   November   Dece

Trace around each student's head (or shine a light on them and trace the shadow) to make a profile silhouette. Give students their silhouettes, magazines, scissors, and glue, and ask them to "fill their heads" with pictures that show who they are. Display.

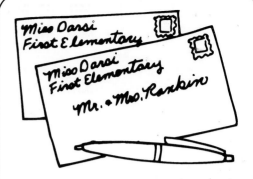

At the end of the first week of school, take time to write a short note to each student's parents, just to give them a few positive comments and to let them know you are in touch with their child as an individual. It will be a good start for effective communication.

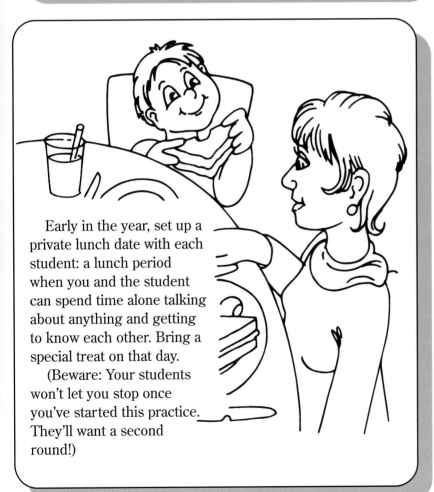

Early in the year, set up a private lunch date with each student: a lunch period when you and the student can spend time alone talking about anything and getting to know each other. Bring a special treat on that day.

(Beware: Your students won't let you stop once you've started this practice. They'll want a second round!)

Get to know your students by having them fill out an informal personal inventory. (Provided on page 69).

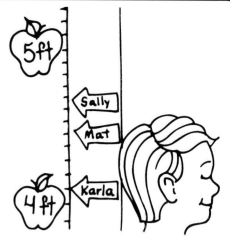

Put up a measuring scale along the wall. (Do one in inches and one in centimeters.) Have students measure one another and mark their heights with arrows. Repeat the measurements midway through the year and at the end to compare heights. Or, students may enjoy graphing their growth every month.

Make a list of 10 promises to yourself: promises to accomplish new things you want to do. Read over your list often.

I Promise to . . .
1) Visit two new schools. 2) Call parents when good things are happening. 3) Take a walk during my lunch hour. 4) Read three professional books before Christmas. 5) Subscribe to a new magazine. 6) Try a new idea once a week. 7) Go somewhere different on a field trip.

Choral reading is a good back-to-school activity because it is a fun, "together" effort. The sense of working together to produce a "choir" effect gives a good group feeling to any class. *Time for Poetry* by Arbuthant is a fine source of poems suitable for choral reading.

About Myself

My name is _____

Today I feel _____

Something special about me is _____

I'd rather _____ than _____

I like teachers that _____

My favorite place to be is _____

Something that bothers me is _____

At our house we _____

Before I go to bed, I like to _____

When I'm alone _____

The most important person in the world is _____

I wish I could _____

Sometimes I like to _____

I think school should be a place where _____

I feel nervous when _____

I wish people wouldn't _____

It makes me angry when _____

Better than anything, I like _____

I really get angry when _____

I feel proud when _____

This year I hope _____

One thing I'd like to know about the teacher is _____

_____

One thing I'd like the teacher to know about me is _____

_____

71

reproducible

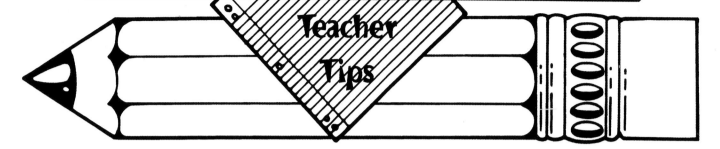

Language Arts

Teacher Tips

Reading Vocabulary Words

As a different approach to learning and displaying vocabulary words, make a vocabulary string mobile. When new words are introduced, each student gets a word and a card. Instruct each student to put the word in large print on one side of the card and a picture showing the meaning of the word on the other side. (This can also include a written definition, if you wish.) Then punch a hole in the bottom and the top of the card and string it on a long shoestring or a piece of yarn with tape wrapped around the end for easier lacing. Students can then stand at the mobiles and practice their words or just see them as they hang in the room.

Springtime Haiku

Teach your students to write haiku by giving them the formula "5-7-5," emphasizing that haiku are usually about nature and stressing that poems don't have to rhyme. Read many examples to them and then write some original ones together.

Later, "pass the hat" containing strips of paper with nature subjects written on them, for example, *cloud, caterpillar, sunbeam, rainbow*, and *nest*. Each student picks one and writes an original haiku on that subject. After the haiku is perfected, have students use construction paper and draw and cut out cherry blossom shapes or shapes symbolic of their subjects. Next, have them neatly copy their haiku onto the cut-outs. Mount the haiku on the branches of a Japanese-style construction-paper cherry tree. (Be sure to explain the significance of cherry trees in the Japanese culture.)

The Three Little "E's" and the Wolf

First make two houses out of shoeboxes. Label one house with an example word that contains the short *e* sound, and label the other house with an example word that contains the long *e* sound. Make cards in the shape of pigs (or use plain cards if time is limited) and write one short *e* or long *e* word on each card. Hold up one card at a time for the class to read. If a student can read and pronounce the word and place it in the correct box, then the "wolf" doesn't get the word. This game can be reused with other vowel and letter sounds.

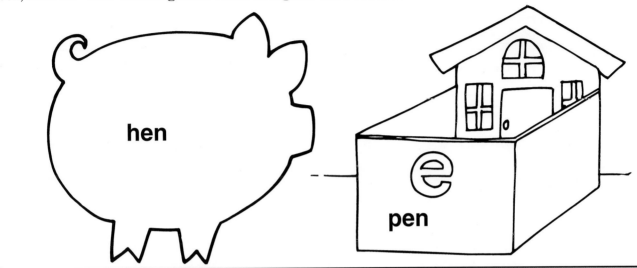

Add-an-Adjective Game

This is a group game that can be used to reinforce adjective or adverb knowledge and use. All that is needed is a chalkboard and chalk!

Directions

To play, a student names one word to start a sentence. The next student says a second word in the sentence, and so on. When one sentence ends, another can be started. Each word is written on the chalkboard. If the word given is an adjective or adverb, the player must say his or her word and then label it with the correct part of speech.

Points are awarded for words that are adjectives or adverbs: one point for adjectives, two points for adverbs. Only three consecutive adjectives or adverbs can be used. One point is subtracted for incorrect labeling. The teacher determines accuracy. The winner is the player with the highest score. Individual or team scores can be kept to see who is the lucky adjective and adverb champion!

Try this game with other parts of speech to reinforce those as well!

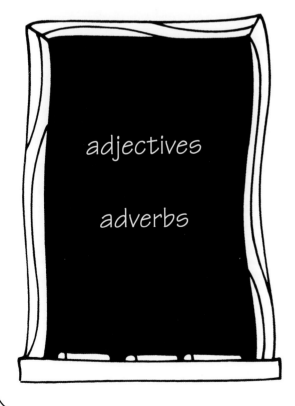

73

Language Arts

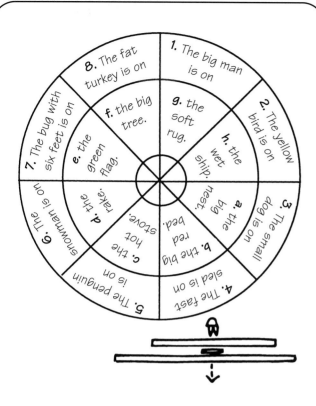

Silly Sentence Picture Wheel

The purpose of this activity is to allow independent phonics practice in which students can show their ability to sound out words.

Materials
- 1 large pizza board
- 1 small pizza board
- markers
- paper fastener
- washer

Method

Each student spins the inner wheel. Then he or she writes down a corresponding number and letter on a piece of drawing paper. (This will enable the teacher to check the drawing at a later time.) The student then sounds out the silly sentence formed by the combined wheels and draws a picture of the sentence. The student's drawing tells the teacher if he or she has correctly sounded out the sentence.

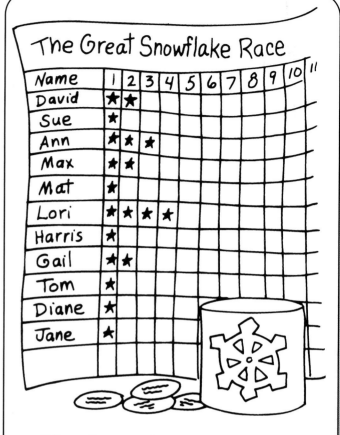

The Great Snowflake Race

For developing an interest in research and encyclopedia usage, have a Great Snowflake Race. Post a chart on the wall with every student's name on it and numbers from 1–50.

Place 50 construction-paper snowflakes in a can. Each snowflake is numbered and contains a question. For example, "Who was the third president of the U.S. and when was he elected to the position?" "Name three requirements for a candidate for the presidency." "Who was the largest president?" "Which president had the most children?" Students must answer each question satisfactorily in order to put a star in the box for that question. The activity is a race to see who can complete all 50 questions first and have all 50 boxes starred beside his or her name on the chart.

(A number of topics can be used for this activity, and it is up to the teacher to come up with questions that will be appropriate for each class.)

Word Walls

Cover an expanse of wall in the classroom with white paper. Ask students to think of compound words which contain the word *moon*. Write them on the wall. Examples: *moonbeam, moonlight, honeymoon,* and so on. Or ask students for words that rhyme with *moon*. Examples: *soon, June, croon,* and so on.

"I Am" Poems

"I Am" poems, in which students write about themselves, are a good exercise to spark an interest in poetry. Place all the poems, unsigned, on a bulletin board and have class members guess the name of the person who they think wrote each poem. Poems should emphasize characteristics and feelings rather than physical descriptions such as tall, short, red hair, and so on.

Stories in Sequence

Writing a class story is interesting and fun. Every writer, whether a great author or just a beginner, writes stories with a beginning, middle, and an end.

Your class can become a collective author with this fun exercise. Give each class member a number, one through the number of students in the class. After the class members have numbers, pass out cards with matching numbers. Number one writes a sentence or paragraph on his or her card and reads it to the class. Number two picks up the story and adds his or her sentence or paragraph. The activity continues until the last student ends the story. When all cards have been read, place them in sequence around the room and leave them up for two or three days for everyone to enjoy.

Create a Snowman

To encourage students to read more during the long winter months, start this project in January. Each student should make the basic form of a snowman (head, middle, body). These pictures are then placed on a wall. Each student must read six books by the first day of spring, and he or she must write a book report on each book. After a report is corrected, each student may add a feature to his or her snowman. The following features can be used.

1st book—eyes

2nd book—nose

3rd book—mouth

4th book—arms

5th book—hat

6th book—scarf

Student Journal

Keeping a journal is a good way to practice putting thoughts on paper. Have students keep a journal or log for one week or more. Here are some ideas to get them started: Write a sentence or two about your family, the weather, what you ate, where you went, your feelings, disappointing or happy events, your best friend, or a new friend.

Word Balloons

Invite students to cut out a balloon shape from construction paper. Instruct students to write their name on their balloon. Display the balloons on a bulletin board. Make a vocabulary list for each student. When a student can read and spell a word correctly for two consecutive days, he or she writes that particular word on a piece of oaktag or a small index card and glues it on his or her balloon. As students fill their balloons, they can take turns reading their words to the class. This will help other students gain new vocabulary as well.

I work in a paper cup factory. My boss wants new uses for paper cups. I think paper cups could be used for . . .

The Creative Writing Challenge

Materials
- several large plastic foam or paper cups on which to write the story starters
- a ditto of a large cup for students to write their stories on

Teacher Directions

Print story starters on cups and tack the cups to the bulletin board. Have the dittoed-cup paper or other paper available.

Student Directions

1. Read the story starters on the cups. Choose one and write a story on the paper that is provided.
2. Put your story in the cup when you are finished.
3. Read a couple of the other stories that are in the cups.

Possible Story Starters

1. The drink in the cup was deep red, cool, and very delicious. I drank half the cup without stopping. Suddenly I felt strange. I looked at my foot and . . .
2. I work in a paper cup factory. My boss wants new uses for paper cups. I think paper cups could be used for . . .
3. The cup was blowing in the wind across the deserted beach. I picked it up and looked inside. My eyes popped, and I screamed as I saw . . .
4. My name is Quarf, and I am from the planet Neptune. As I step out of my spaceship, I find a paper cup. I look with my photo eyes, and I can see everywhere this cup has been. This is what I see . . .

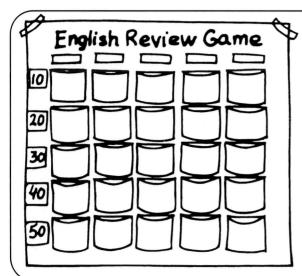

English Review Game

Cut 13 regular-sized white envelopes in half and glue them onto a large sheet of posterboard, making five rows of five envelope halves. Number each row 10, 20, 30, 40, and 50 to designate point value. List five different categories on the board above the columns of envelopes: Dictionary; Parts of Speech; Poetry; Capitalization and Punctuation; and Take a Chance.

Questions ranging in difficulty are written on index cards, which are then placed in the envelope pockets. Make some questions bonus questions (double points). Teams compete by choosing any category and point value. The winner is the team with the most points.

Language Arts

The Spelling Challenge

Teacher Directions

Put current spelling list words or other spelling words on cups (10–15 words). Spell the word correctly on one cup and spell it incorrectly on another cup. Set the cups side by side. Have students place a straw in the cup with the correctly spelled word.

Student Directions

Place a straw in every cup with a correctly spelled word printed on it. Do not put straws in the cups with incorrectly spelled words.

Possible Spelling Starters

rabbit-rabit
hitting-hiting
picture-picksure
double-doubel
library-librery
parties-partys
enough-enuff
knife-nife
taking-takeing
giggling-giggleing
said-siad
cheer-chear

ABC Challenge

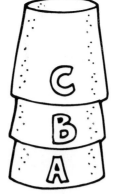

Teacher Directions

Print words on 24 cups. Use sight words, a current spelling or vocabulary list, or use the challenging list below. Stack the cups in random order. Have students unstack the cups and restack them in ABC order.

Student Directions

Restack the cups, putting the words in ABC order. The "A" word will be on the bottom.

Possible Word List

appropriate	beneficial	courteous	delicious
extraterrestrial	ferocious	generous	horrible
juicy	kindred	likable	magnificent
numerous	omnipotent	pleasant	quickly
rational	sensational	terrific	universal
wonderful	young		

Name That Character!

Put your budding young detectives to work guessing the identity of popular book characters. The characters can either be people or animals. Here is a list of ideas: Heidi, Alice in Wonderland, Cinderella, Miss Nelson, Mary Poppins, Curious George, Winnie the Pooh, Babar, Clifford the Big Red Dog, and Corduroy. Write each book character's name on a small index card. Divide your class into teams of four or five students and have a team captain choose one of the character cards. (Ssh! It's a secret!) Have each team meet quietly and write five one-word clues about the character or book. For example, clue words for Cinderella could be: ball, pumpkin, stepmother, work, prince. Set an appropriate time limit for the teams to meet.

When time is up, have a sharing time. Let the audience guess the mystery characters by using the clues given by each team.

Learning Centers

Teacher Tips

Chilly Chores

Using the snowman pattern and the activities found below, make a wintertime learning center for your classroom.

Reproduce the pattern and type or write one activity on each snowman. Laminate for lasting durability.

- If Frosty the Snowman came to your house to spend the day, what are some things that you would do?
- Describe and draw a new invention that removes snow from the sidewalk without using a shovel.
- Make a list of all the different board games you can think of that would be fun to play in the winter.
- Make a list of all the winter sports you can think of.
- Make a word search containing at least 20 words that pertain to winter.
- Design a snowman using plastic foam pieces. Name it and write a short poem about it.
- Write five synonyms for *cold*. Write five antonyms for *cold*. Choose one of each and use them in a winter sentence.
- Pick your favorite winter sport and write directions for playing it. Read your directions to a friend and see if he or she can draw a picture using your directions.
- Use the encyclopedia to find out how snowflakes are formed. Design one of your own on paper and cut it out.
- List 20 words that remind you of winter.

ACTIVITY IDEAS TO GET YOU STARTED

Hello

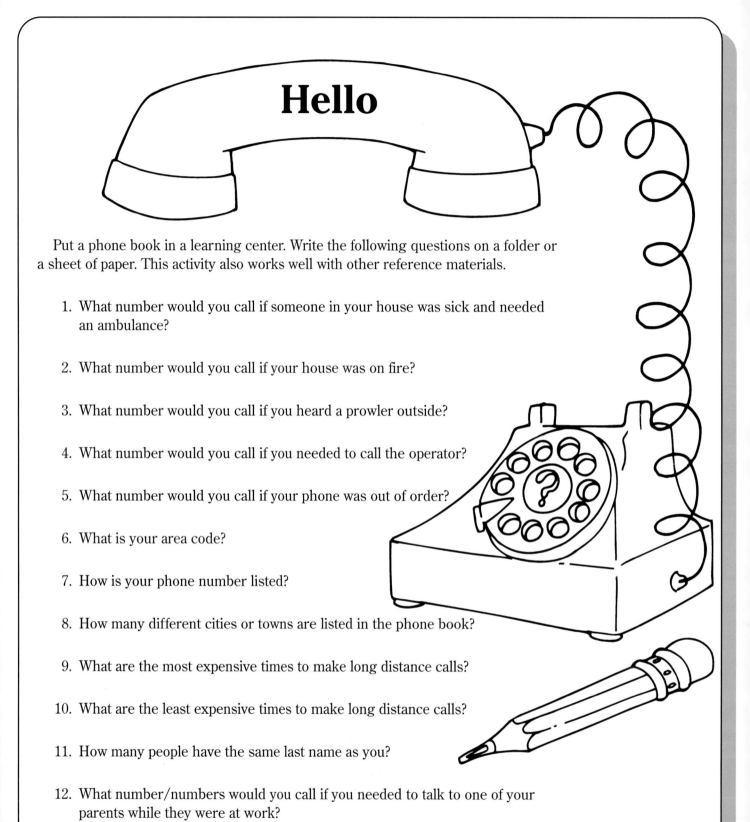

Put a phone book in a learning center. Write the following questions on a folder or a sheet of paper. This activity also works well with other reference materials.

1. What number would you call if someone in your house was sick and needed an ambulance?

2. What number would you call if your house was on fire?

3. What number would you call if you heard a prowler outside?

4. What number would you call if you needed to call the operator?

5. What number would you call if your phone was out of order?

6. What is your area code?

7. How is your phone number listed?

8. How many different cities or towns are listed in the phone book?

9. What are the most expensive times to make long distance calls?

10. What are the least expensive times to make long distance calls?

11. How many people have the same last name as you?

12. What number/numbers would you call if you needed to talk to one of your parents while they were at work?

Canned Questions and Answers

This activity can be used for individual students, group research, class involvement within one discipline, or within the context of many subject areas you are covering in class.

Purchase a case or two of canning jars. Decide what fruits and/or vegetables you want to "can" for this activity. Choose construction paper in colors similar to the colors of the real fruits and/or vegetables you have chosen for this activity (example: purple for grapes, yellow for corn, and so on). Decide on a place in your classroom that can be used as the "pantry."

Outline the shapes of your chosen vegetables and/or fruits. Make them large enough to write questions on but small enough to fit into your canning jars. Cut out each one and write questions, directions, math problems, and so on, on each. Each piece of fruit can have one activity or question, or if you are dealing with one article or story, more than one question can be written. If possible, laminate each piece of fruit and/or vegetable before placing it in the jar. (Label each piece with a different letter or number.)

Place the fruit and/or vegetables in the jars and arrange them on the "pantry" shelf. Perhaps you would want to label each jar with titles such as *Corny Questions*, or *Grape Research Activities*. Use your imagination.

Next, design a worksheet that students will use to write their answers on when they have completed their research. Perhaps an outline of a large jar with lines drawn on the front would work.

Place several copies of the worksheet in the pantry area. Students then choose a jar, pick a fruit or vegetable, and answer the question. Make sure that students label each answer sheet with the letter or number you have used to label the fruit. This will keep a record of the fruits and vegetables "eaten."

Have students line up their answer "jars" on a bulletin board or in a straight line on a wall of the classroom. Share and discuss the results when time permits.

Category Game

To help students become more aware of words that denote categories, as well as words that make up categories, try this game. Choose three students to play together. One student holds a set of alphabet cards and names the categories. Having a set list of categories on hand makes the game go smoother. The other two students vie with each other to be the first to call out a word that falls into the category and begins with the letter the cardholder holds up. For example, the cardholder calls out the category "Vegetable" while holding up the B card. The other two students race with each other to name a vegetable that starts with the letter B. They could say *bean*, *broccoli*, or *beet*. The first player who gives an appropriate word beginning with the shown letter and in the stated category receives a point. The player who gets the most points during the playing time wins the game.

This game calls for quick thinking and recall. Some students begin to look in their dictionaries for unusual and different words to spring on their classmates. They become more word conscious and increase the number of words in their vocabularies.

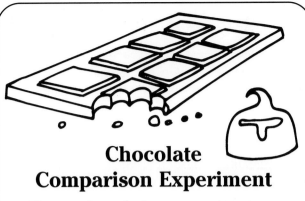

Chocolate Comparison Experiment

Have students devise an experiment or survey in which they test various brands of chocolate for taste, appearance, smell, and so on. Have them conduct their experiment and report the results, using graphs and charts, to show what they have discovered.

Charlie and the Chocolate Factory

Have students read or listen to excerpts from *Charlie and the Chocolate Factory* by Roald Dahl. Have them use Charlie as the main character in a cooperative story, adding another chapter to the book.

How Chocolate Came to Be

At this center, include information about how chocolate really came to be. Also include examples of myths and legends that explain how the bear got its short tail or how the turtle got its shell or how thunder was invented. Invite students to brainstorm many varied and unusual explanations for how chocolate came to be. Have them create a script for their most original idea and act it out for the class.

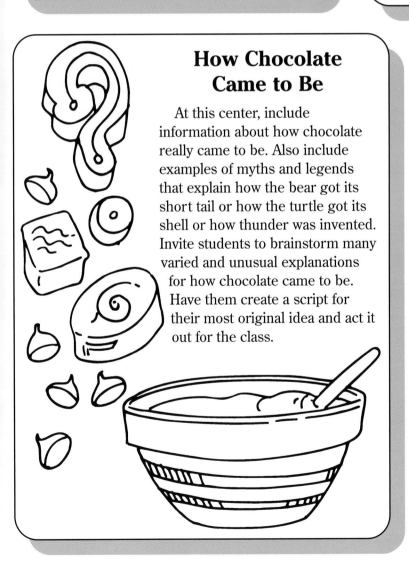

It's a New Taste Sensation

At this center, provide examples of a wide variety of chocolate products. Instruct students to create their own original chocolate products and design an ad campaign for selling these products. Videotape their finished ads. Have students vote on the videos and award a prize for the top new chocolate product.

Popcorn Galore!

At this center, invite students to work together to brainstorm all the possible varieties of popcorn they can create. Have them list these varieties. Then have students select the best idea and prepare a marketing plan for this new, improved popcorn.

Popcorn Critics

At this center, have several varieties of popcorn kernels. Have students sort these in as many ways as they can. Have them use hoops to do the sorting and use Venn diagrams to show their results. Have students share these results with the rest of the class. Scales, magnifying glasses, various measuring utensils, and other devices should be placed at this center. A popcorn popper should also be on hand so that students can test their predictions about the best popping results by using small quantities of each variety.

100 Creative Ways to Use Popcorn!

In this center, invite students to stretch their creative thinking skills by brainstorming a list of at least 100 things to do with popcorn—besides eating it! They may make the popcorn larger, smaller, glue it together, and combine it with other things to come up with new ideas!

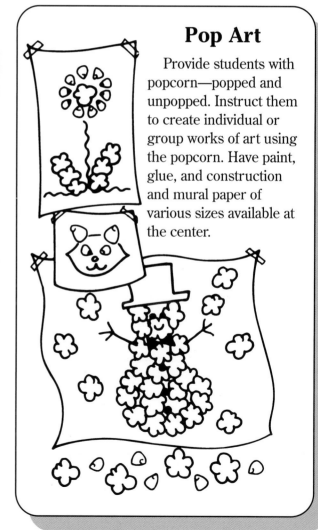

Pop Art

Provide students with popcorn—popped and unpopped. Instruct them to create individual or group works of art using the popcorn. Have paint, glue, and construction and mural paper of various sizes available at the center.

Math

One Stands Alone

Materials
- 3" × 5" (8 × 13 cm) index cards
- paper fastener
- oaktag
- scissors
- various colors of construction paper

Write a riddle or a math story problem on each card. Make three 1/2" × 3" (1.25 × 8 cm) strips from oaktag for each card. Secure these strips to the right side of the index card with a paper fastener. Use various colors of construction paper and make flower shapes. On these flower shapes, write three answers to the question which is written on the index card. The student reads the problem, raises the three flower strips, and chooses one answer. If correct, an "X" will be on the back of the flower shape. One flower strip will stand and the other two will be folded in back of the card.

Toothpick Geometric Figure Race

- Give each student 10 toothpicks. Call out a geometric figure, such as "pentagon." The first student to make a correct pentagon scores a point. The student with the most points wins.

- Or, divide class into teams of five students each. There can be as many teams as necessary. Call out a geometric shape, such as "hexagon." First team to form the shape scores a point.

- Give each student 10 toothpicks. Have each student make a shape as you call it out. There is no contest nor points scored.

- Shapes that can be used, depending on the sophistication of students, include the following: square, triangle, quadrilateral, polygon, right angle, acute angle, obtuse angle, perpendicular lines, parallel lines, hexagon, octagon, and decagon.

Math

	Total
Week 1	37¢
Week 2	14¢
Week 3	52¢
Week 4	
Week 5	

Mathematics

Gather or save large shopping bags from a local market. Divide the class into small groups of two or three to decorate each bag with a spring theme. When bags are completed, tape them to the chalkboard ledge or hang them on a bulletin board low enough for students to reach. Tell them that these bags will be like the wishing wells used in England. (Send notes home so that parents are informed of the project. Ask if they can send just a few pennies for the wishing wells. Explain that the money will be given to the homeless or another charity in your area.) At the end of each day, have students count the amount of money in the bags and record these on a large wall graph. At the end of the week, have students add the entire amount collected. Discuss where they think the money should be donated.

Even and Odd Numbers

After discussing even and odd numbers, use the math activities described below to develop worksheets to help reinforce the skill. One idea is to draw several circles on a sheet of paper with three- or four-digit numbers in each of them. Then give the following directions: Add all the even numbers and then add all the odd numbers. Subtract the smaller number from the larger number to find the difference. Alternate directions: Color the even numbers a certain color and the odd numbers another color. These directions could also be combined into one activity sheet rather than two.

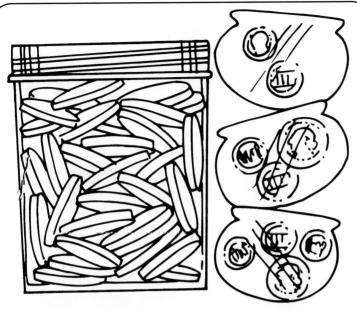

How Much in a Pot of Gold?

Fill a peanut butter jar with pennies. Have students guess the correct number of pennies in the jar. Five new pennies will make a nice prize for the winner. This is an excellent lead-in to a discussion of estimation.

If you have students who have mastered the concept of counting coins, here are some questions that will send them off to the library for some old-fashioned research. Entitle this activity Search for Gold.

- What does 14, 18, and 24 karat gold mean?
- How are gold coins made and where are they made?
- What was the Gold Rush?

Give students practice in counting money by using paper pots of gold. Cut out 10 pots from sheets of golden colored construction paper. On each paper pot, stamp a variety of coins. Use coin stamps and a stamp pad to make this task easy. Place all the completed "pots of gold" in a pocket folder. Be sure to number each pot. Ask students to count the money in each pot. In the pocket folder can also be duplicated answer sheets (one for each student to complete) and a pencil. An answer key listing the total amount in each pot can also be provided to make this a self-checking activity.

Laminate each pot after the coins have been stamped. The entire activity can be stored in a small flat box.

Some pots of gold could be labeled with money story problems such as "How much money would be left in the pot if you spent one dollar?" Students would then write the amount of change on their answer sheets.

Super Thinker

Super Thinker is a game to play in math class. It is a nice way to provide a break in the routine. Simply say, "It's time to play Super Thinker." Then draw the outline of a head on the chalkboard.

Give students a series of numbers to add, subtract, multiply, or divide in their heads. Each student should write each answer on paper. Walk around the room and check the answers or call for hands of those who are correct as you write the answer on the board.

Next, write the names of the students who had the correct answer inside the head shape. Students enjoy this break, even those who find math difficult to deal with. It is a fun way to drill facts. If a student is correct more than once, place hash marks next to his or her name.

Math

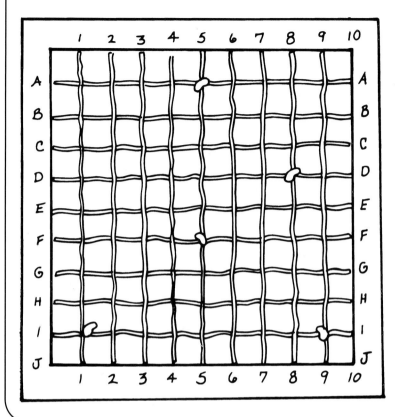

Make a String Graph

Materials

- construction paper
- string
- scissors
- ruler
- pencil
- beans (pinto, lima, and so on) or noodles

Made by Mary
A,5   D,8
F,5   I,I   I,9

Give each student a piece of graph paper with large gridlines. Instruct students to label their grids vertically and horizontally as shown at left. Tell students to cut string the length of the gridlines and glue it right on top of each line. Then have students glue beans or noodles at various coordinates. Let the grids dry overnight. Invite students to make labels that have their names and list the coordinates of their beans. Display the graphs along with the students' labels.

Roll a Product

Each player will need a game board like the one illustrated. Create four dice from wooden cubes. Two should be numbered 0, 1, 2, 3, 4, and 5 with a blue marker. The other two cubes should be numbered 0, 6, 7, 8, 9, and 10 with a red marker. Provide dried beans or pennies to use as game markers.

To start, each player rolls a red die. The one with the largest number is the first player. In turn, the player selects and rolls two dice. The product of the two numbers shown on the top faces is covered on the game board. If the product is already covered, the player loses a chance to cover a square. Play continues in this manner until one player has six markers in a horizontal row or seven markers in a vertical row.

Roll a Product

1	50	60	70	80	90
0	2	3	4	5	6
7	8	9	10	12	14
15	16	18	20	21	24
25	27	28	30	32	35
36	40	42	45	48	49
54	56	63	64	72	81

Math

Pair Up for Math Fun

Let students pair off to solve problems in two-digit addition and subtraction. The first student adds or subtracts the ones column, the second student, the tens. Colored pencils make this activity more fun. Score a point for each example worked correctly. Which pair in the classroom can work most accurately? Expand this idea to include three- and four-digit numbers as well as multiplication and division.

Times Champ

Make a game board like the one below. You will also need two sets of markers, each a different color. On each set of markers, write the products made by multiplying the numbers on the game board. The completed markers should be separated according to color. Each player receives a set.

Play begins with each pile of markers turned facedown. Each player, in turn, picks a marker, turns it over and reads the product. The player then places the marker on the playing board in the correct box. If the player cannot do this, the marker is set aside, and it is the next player's turn.

A player may challenge an opponent's placement. If the marker is in the wrong box, it must be removed and put on the bottom of the pile. It is the next player's turn. If the player was correct, the opponent loses his or her next turn.

The game stops when no more markers can be played. The winner is the person with the most markers on the board, or when a specified amount of time is up.

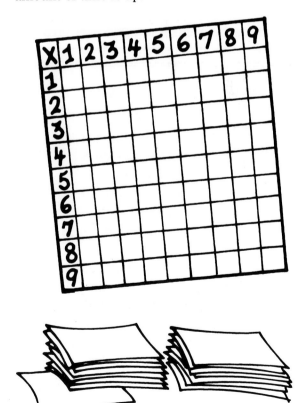

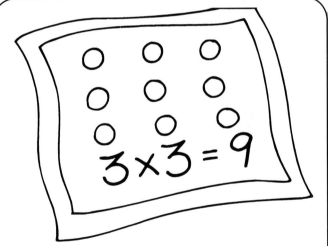

Wholly Number Facts

To illustrate a number fact, have each student write the fact on a piece of construction paper and use a paper punch to make holes to illustrate the fact. Mount the papers on a contrasting background. Display on a bulletin board, or punch a hole in each and tie with yarn for a booklet.

91

Ice Melt Mania

Your class will "warm up" to this icy estimating activity! Prepare a tray of ice cubes tinted with blue food coloring. Provide each team of students with a small, clear glass jar or bowl; a spoon; and a stopwatch. Challenge each group to estimate the number of minutes or seconds that it will take for a blue ice cube to melt when placed in a jar or bowl containing hot water. Invite groups to write their estimates on a piece of paper. Fill each jar or bowl with hot water before dropping a blue ice cube into it. Have one student in each group use the stopwatch to measure the passing time. Students may stir the water with the spoon to speed up the melting process, or just sit and watch as the cube dissolves. Instruct students to press STOP on their stopwatches when the cube has completely melted. Help teams to find the difference between their estimates and the actual melting times. List the differences on a chart. Identify the three smallest differences. Discuss which teams used their spoons. Award the appropriate number of snowballs (marshmallows) to each winning team.

Scoring Points
Smallest Difference—first: 3 snowballs; second: 2 snowballs; third: 1 snowball

The Great Snowball Grab

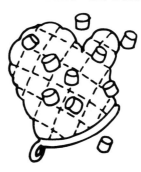

A large bowl of mini marshmallows and a thick, colorful mitten are all you'll need for this exciting estimating activity! Provide each student with a 5" × 5" (13 × 13 cm) piece of paper, split by a diagonal line. Challenge students to estimate the number of "snowballs" (mini marshmallows) that they will be able to grab while wearing the mitten. Ask students to write their estimates above the diagonal line on their pages. The fun begins as each student steps forward, puts on the mitten, reaches into the bowl, and grabs as many snowballs as possible. Only one grab is permitted. The competitors must have a firm hold on their snowballs before being allowed to drop the handfuls onto paper plates set beside the bowl. As a class, count each plate of snowballs, then have each student record his or her tally below the diagonal line on the paper. Students should then calculate the difference between their estimates and the actual number of snowballs grabbed from the bowl. Invite students to share their answers. Identify the three students with the smallest differences. Also recognize the three students who were able to grab the greatest number of snowballs. Award the appropriate number of snowballs (marshmallows) to each team.

Scoring Points
Smallest Difference—first: 3 snowballs; second: 2 snowballs; third: 1 snowball
Greatest Grab—first: 3 snowballs; second: 2 snowballs; third: 1 snowball

Snow Shoveling Estimation

Snow removal has never been so much fun! Display three large, clear glass jars in a variety of sizes and shapes. Fill each jar with "snow" (flour). Pass several "snow shovels" (teaspoons) around the classroom for students to examine. Challenge students to estimate the number of "shovels" full of "snow" in each of the three jars. After the estimates have been recorded on paper, invite the class to help with the shoveling. Encourage students to think of timesaving methods that may be used to measure the amount of snow in the jars. Discuss each suggestion. Be sure to have a set of measuring cups standing by. One clever snow shoveler is sure to suggest identifying the number of teaspoons in one cup and then using the cup to remove and measure the snow. Work together to empty the snow from jars 1, 2, and 3. Ask the class to identify the difference between their three estimates and the actual number of shovels in each jar. Identify the three students who had the smallest differences for each jar. Award the appropriate number of snowballs (marshmallows) to each team.

Scoring Points

Smallest Difference—Jar 1: first: 3 snowballs; second: 2 snowballs; third: 1 snowball. **Jar 2:** first: 3 snowballs; second: 2 snowballs; third: 1 snowball. **Jar 3:** first: 3 snowballs; second: 2 snowballs; third: 1 snowball

93

Index

A

ABC challenge activity, 80
About myself activity, 70–71
Activities
    about myself, 70–71
    choral reading, 70
    class crest, 68
    "fill their heads," 69
    get-to-know-you, 13
    ideas, 67–95
    measuring scale, 70
    poetry, 19
    private lunch date, 69
    setting goal, 68
    sponge, 17
    10 promises, 70
    time line, 68
    warm-up, for first day, 11
    See also Language arts activities;
        Language centers activities;
        Math activities
Add-an-adjective game, 73
Arbuthant, 70
Assembly, 55
Assessment, 47–49

B

Behavior
    during assembly, 55
    daily, contract for, 38
    during field trip, 54
    managing, 32–38
    rewarding appropriate, 32–33
    sharing positive messages with
        parents about, 33
Books to read aloud, 18
Bulletin board, 5–7
    displaying student work on, 5
    We're Proud of Our Work, 8

C

Canned questions and answers
  activity, 84
Category game, 84
Centers, 46. *See also* Learning centers
  activities

Charlie and the Chocolate Factory
  activity, 85
Checklist
    building relationships, 42
    designing classroom for day's
        lesson, 52
    designing your classroom, 10
    handling emergencies, 60
    managing student behavior, 37
    organizing classroom with rules
        and procedures, 29
    successful start, 16
Chilly chores activity, 81
Chocolate comparison experiment, 85
Chocolate history, 85
Choral reading activity, 70
Class crest activity, 68
Class list, 12, 20
Classroom
    bulletin board, 5–8
    clean, 7–8
    designing your, 5–10
    organizing, with clear rules and
        procedures, 21–31
    personal space in, 6–7
    seating arrangement, 7
    Tips from Teachers, 9
    traffic pattern, 6
    See also Rules and procedures
contract, Daily behavior, 38
Creative writing challenge activity, 78

D

Daily behavior contract, 38
daily tasks, Rules and procedures for,
  21–22
Dismissal, 12
Displaying student work, 5

E

emergency, Checklist for handling, 60
End of day
    rules and procedures for, 23
    Tips from Teachers on, 28
English review game, 78
Equity card, 46

Evaluation
    for lesson plan, 53
    See also Assessment, 53
Even and odd numbers activity, 88
Events, 54–61
    assembly, 55
    dealing with unexpected, 57–58
    field trip, 54–55
    fire drill, 58
    parent visitation, 55–56
    party/indoor recess, 56
    substitutes, 57–58
    teaching observation, 57
    Tips from Teachers on, 59

F

Field trip, 54–55
    behavior expectations during, 54
    permission slip for, 61
"Fill their heads" activity, 69
Fire drill, 58
First days, 11–16
    assessing students' abilities on, 13
    checklist, 16
    class list, 12
    emergency phone number list, 12
    establishing classroom rules and
        procedures, 12
    getting students home, 12
    get-to-know-you activities, 13
    name tags, 11
    supply list, 11
    warm-up activity, 11

G

Great snowball grab activity, 92
Great snowflake race activity, 74
Groups, 47

H

home, Getting students, 12
homework, System for recording,
  24–25

I

"I am" poem activity, 75
Ice melt mania activity, 92
illness, Student, 58
injury, Student, 58
Instruction
    assessment, 47–49
    centers for, 46
    delivering, 45–47
    equity card, 46
    planning, 44–45
    See also Lesson

J

journal activity, Student, 77

K

Keys. *See* Checklist

L

Language arts activities, 72–80
    add-an-adjective game, 73
    canned questions and answers, 84
    category game, 85
    create a snowman, 76
    creative writing challenge, 79
    English review game, 79
    great snowflake race, 74
    "I am" poem, 75
    reading vocabulary words, 72
    silly sentence picture wheel, 74
    springtime haiku, 72
    stories in sequence, 75
    student journal, 77
    Three Little "E's" and the Wolf, 73
    word balloons, 77
    word walls, 75
Learning centers activities, 81–86
    ABC challenge, 79
    Charlie and the Chocolate Factory, 85
    chilly chores, 81
    chocolate comparison experiment, 85
    chocolate history, 85
    name that character, 80
    phone book, 82
    popcorn, 86
    spelling challenge, 79
    taste sensation, 85

Lesson
    bringing closure to, 47
    checklist for designing classroom for day's, 52
    finding resources for, 45
    keys to well-developed, 44–45
    long-range plan, 44
    planning, 44–50
    preparing for, 45
    short-range plan, 44
Lesson plan evaluation, 53
lunch date activity, Private, 69

M

Managing supplies, 15
Math activities, 87–93
    even and odd numbers, 88
    great snowball grab, 92
    ice melt mania, 92
    one stands alone, 87
    pair up for math fun, 91
    pot of gold, 89
    roll a product, 90
    snow shoveling estimation, 93
    string graph, 90
    super thinker, 89
    times champ, 91
    toothpick geometric figure race, 87
    wholly number facts, 91
    wishing wells, 88
Measuring scale activity, 70
Mentor, finding, 39
Misbehavior, 33–35

N

Name tag, 11
Name that character activity, 80

O

Observation, teaching, 57
One stands alone activity, 87
Organization, professional, 63

P

Pair up for math fun activity, 91
Parents
    dealing with problems, 40
    developing relations with, 40–41
    note to, 69

    sharing positive messages about behavior with, 33
    visitation, 55–56
Parent-teacher conference, 40
    notification of, 43
Party, 56
Personal space, in classroom, 6–7
Phone book activity, 83
phone number list, Emergency, 12
Pinch card, 47
Planning
    first day, 11–16
    lessons, 44–50
    Tips from Teachers on, 50
Poetry activities, 19, 75
Popcorn activity, 86
Portfolio, 48
Pot of gold activity, 89
Procedures. *See* Rules and procedures
Progress note. *See* Report card

R

reading aloud, Books for, 13, 18
Recess, indoor, 56
Report card, 49
Reward
    for appropriate behavior, 32–33
    Tips from Teachers on, 35
Roll a product activity, 90
Rules and procedures, 12
    absent students, 25
    checklist, 29
    create, 21
    daily tasks, 21–22
    end of day, 23
    field trip, 54
    organizing classroom with, 21–31
    reproducible sample of, for room, 30–31
    for start of day, 23
    system for recording homework, 24–25
    tips for establishing, 21
    Tips from Teachers, 26–27
    for transition times, 23

S

Seating arrangement, in classroom, 7
Silly sentence picture wheel activity, 74
Snowman activity, 76

Snow shoveling estimation activity, 93
Spelling challenge activity, 79
Sponge activities, 17
Springtime haiku activity, 72
staff, Developing relations with, 39, 41
Start of day
    rules and procedures for, 23
    Tips from Teachers on, 27
Stories in sequence activity, 75
String graph activity, 90
Student of the Week, 5
Students
    assessing abilities of, 13
    behavior during assembly, 55
    behavior expectations on field trip, 54
    developing relations with, 39–41
    displaying work of, 5
    getting them home, 12
    getting to know your, 13
    illness, 58
    injury, 58
    journal activity, 77
    managing behavior of, 32–38
    personal space and, 6–7

Substitute teacher, 57–58
Super thinker activity, 89
Supplies, 15

T

Taste sensation activity, 85
Teaching
    joys and challenges of, 62–66
    Tips from Teachers on enjoying, 64
Ten promises activity, 70
Three Little "E's" and the Wolf
    activity, 73
Time for Poetry, 70
Time line activity, 68
Times champ activity, 91
Tips for establishing rules and
    procedures, 21
Tips from Teachers
    building relationships, 41
    consequences of misbehavior, 36
    cooperative learning, 51
    designing your classroom, 9
    end of day, 28
    enjoying your career, 64

first week's activities, 14–15
getting to know each other, 14
managing supplies, 15
planning, 50
rewards, 35
rules and procedures, 26–27
special events, 59
start of day, 27
Toothpick geometric figure race, 87
traffic pattern, Classroom, 6
Transition time, rules and procedures
    for, 23

V

Vocabulary words activity, reading, 72

W

Warm-up activity, 11
Wholly number facts activity, 91
Wishing wells activity, 88
Word balloons activity, 77
Word walls activity, 75